P9-BYZ-745

mime

a playbook of silent fantasy

 A Headlands Press Book

mime
a playbook of silent fantasy

Kay Hamblin

photographs by
Andrew Fluegelman

Dolphin Books   Doubleday & Company, Inc.   Garden City, New York

CICERO PUBLIC LIBRARY

Created and produced by
The Headlands Press, Inc.,
San Francisco, California

Copyright ©1978 by Kay Hamblin
and The Headlands Press, Inc.

All rights reserved. No portion of this
book may be reproduced—
mechanically, electronically, or by any
other means, including
photocopying, recording, or by
information storage or retrieval
systems—without permission in
writing from Doubleday & Company,
Inc., 245 Park Avenue, New York,
New York 10017.

Photograph on page 16 reprinted by
permission of The Museum of
Modern Art Film Stills Archive, New
York, New York.

Library of Congress
Cataloging in Publication Data

Hamblin, Kay, 1941–
Mime: a playbook of silent fantasy.
"A Headlands Press book."
Bibliography: p. 189.
Includes index.
Summary: Essays introduce mime as
an expressive and recreational activity
and instructions are given for many
exercises and gestures of this silently
communicative art form.
1. Mime.   [1. Pantomime]
I. Fluegelman, Andrew, 1943–
II. Title.
PN2071.G4H3   792.3   78-5545
ISBN 0-385-14246-3

792.3
IfAM

792152

To Basil, Colin, and Seth
and our fantasy life.

Contents

Acknowledge-
ments

There's an understandable difficulty in trying to *write* about mime. When words seem to get in the way, I visualize some of the special moments over the last six years that have taught me about mime as communication:

That first mime troupe of teenagers, performing at a party to benefit the Marin Symphony. The performance was infectious; the guests—adults and children—wanted to play, too. As they dabbed on whiteface, talk disappeared and communication increased. We all moved and mingled in the sunlight for another hour, bumping into each other's illusions, sharing a silent romp.

A street performance in Florence, where the tug-of-war stretched across the Piazza d'Espagne and the 'spectators', middle-aged men, joined in, pulling, puffing, clapping each other on the shoulder when they won possession of the illusory rope. More wanted to play. We created a bus—a *big* bus—that careened around the square, going nowhere and everywhere.

The Laterna Magica in Prague and the Czech mimes at the Avignon Festival in 1977. Every gesture was subject to interpretation: personal, political, powerful. How wonderfully difficult it is to prosecute statements that vanish into thin air!

The lawyers, doctors, carpenters, roofers, jazz musicians, computer programmers, therapists, teachers, surfers, and grandparents who have made my classes come alive, and who shared their time and creativity to become the Mimes of this book. Some have gone on to performance and further study; others went home to play with their children.

These are only part of a great collection. I don't remember all the names, but the fantasies are indelible.

A special thanks to Margaret and Adolph for fostering illusion; Karl Bissenger for introducing me to theatre for people and politics; Anna Halprin for moving my teaching in that direction; the College of Marin for making my classes available to people of all ages; Sylvia Boorstein for the suggestion; Barry Traub for his vision and confidence; Bruce and Maiga Dayton for the garret; Bari Rolfe for sharing her knowledge and resources; Shoshana Tembeck for her care with my words; Howard Jacobsen for his graphic visualizations; San Domenico School for granting me space and support; Baron Wolman and William Piltzer for their generous loan of equipment; Lester Barnett for his talent and commitment; Ayat Cate for her playful spirit; all the Mimes for their shared energy; and to Andrew Fluegelman for making illusion into reality.

K.H.
April 1978

The Mimes

Kent Baldwin
Jesse Barnett
Lester Barnett
Russell Barnett
Bernie Barrish
Frances Barrish
David Boucke
Eric Bram
Fred Burke
Salvatore Busalacchi
Gabrielle Carteris
Ayat Cate
Mary Chamberlin
Wesley Chamberlin
Christina Cortese
Sherre David
Nancy Edelson
Kay Elmore
Bob Engan
Kim Englebright
Andrew Fluegelman
Kirk Frederick
Robin Frederick
Gina Friedlander
Russell Fuller
Laurie Guerin
Basil Hamblin
Colin Hamblin
Kay Hamblin
Seth Hamblin
Malcolm Hamilton
Reed Hamilton
Jon Harris
Katie Harrison
Carrie Jacobson
David Jenkins
Melanie Jenkins
Grant Kalinowski
Tracy Kanbara
Steve Karman
Jeff Katz
David Kern
Neil King
Denise Kirchner
Ann Krinitsky
Dian Lyons

Alex McKleroy
Callie McLellan
Jennifer Massen
Yann Michel
David Myles
Ellan Nance
Bill Nerenberg
Cindy Norton
Julia Reinertsen
Carlos Resas
Mary Beth Richardson
Danny Rodrigues
Piper Ross
John Rubin
Lacy Rumsey
Ellen Sander
Jamie Seidel
Elina Shacklett
Robbie Sherman
Jean Singer
Jon Sperry
Jay Strickler
Andrew Susac
Shoshana Tembeck
Mike Watters
Peggy Watters
Doug Whitney
Jerry Winston
Andy Zlot

INTRODUCTION
Mime as Play

Would you like to fly?
Would you like to be two people?
Would you like to own a magic lamp?
You can. There's a mime inside you, and with mime, anything is possible. All you need are your body and your imagination, and they're with you all the time.

Mime is creating fantasy with illusion. Perhaps it's your personal fantasy, perhaps a universally shared fantasy. As your body shapes the illusion, the fantasy becomes reality—for you, and for anyone who's watching.

Mime is silent communication—talking without words. Instead of using your voice, you're using your entire self to express your ideas. Mime is a language the whole world understands.

Mime is an art, but you need not think of yourself as an artist, or even a performer, to enjoy and share mime with your friends. Mime is a game that everyone can play.

The Mime Tradition

Some form of mime has been with us since the first cave people acted out their experiences of the hunt. The Greeks used mime in religious ceremonies. The Romans staged popular mime performances in the arena and made mimes the priests of Apollo. During the Middle Ages, mime remained a part of religious instruction, particularly in mystery, miracle, and morality plays. In the sixteenth century, mime was brought back to the stage and into the streets for pure entertainment in the form of the Italian *commedia dell'arte*, with its cast of stock characters, one of which was Pierrot, the clown/fool.

Popular mime as we know it, however, began in the early nineteenth century with the work of Jean Gaspard 'Baptiste' Deburau at the Theatre des Funambles in Paris. Deburau changed mime from slapstick to theatre. He created stories with realistic scenes, character development, and plots about everyday life.

Marcel Carne's film *Les Enfants du Paradis* (*Children of Paradise*) is a fictional biography of Deburau and his rise from a simple, itinerant clown to one of the world's most famous Pierrots. In this film appear two of the greatest French mimes: Jean-Louis Barrault (as Deburau) and Etienne Decroux (as Deburau's father).

Etienne Decroux was a master teacher as well as a mime. Based on his 'statuary' studies in Paris in the 1920s, Decroux created theories, exercises, and specific mimetic illusions which he taught his students and which have become the basis for much mime technique. One of these students has become far more famous than his teacher, inspiring an

Jean-Louis Barrault as Deburau in the film 'Children of Paradise'

international enthusiasm for mime. He is Marcel Marceau.

Usually appearing as a solitary white-faced individual on a bare stage, Marceau has performed to capacity audiences around the world, in theaters, and on the global stage of television. His performances present 'style pantomimes' which deal symbolically with such themes as creation, evolution, and justice, and a series of Pierrot-like adventures of his special character Bip. Bip is Everyman. Bip looks for a job, attends parties, goes to war, falls in love—even commits suicide (or tries

to!). The influence on Marceau of American silent movie stars Charlie Chaplin, Buster Keaton, and Stan Laurel is particularly evident when Bip plays the poor soul or the rejected suitor. Whatever diverse influences Marceau has absorbed during his years of celebrating life through illusion, they are minor compared to the influence he continues to have on other mimes as a performer and a teacher.

Today the mime tradition reflects varied styles around the world, from the Zen quality of the Japanese Mamako Yoneyama to the inventive body abstractions of the Mummenshanz Swiss Mime Mask

Theater. Some mimes have remained close to the tradition of the circus, such as Switzerland's Dimitri and Czechoslovakia's Polívka and Turba.

Many Americans have been introduced to mime firsthand by the recent revival of the street-performing tradition. Like the mimes, acrobats, and clowns that have toured Europe for centuries, modern street mimes rely on their talent and wit to capture and captivate audiences from the passing crowd. Robert Shields, who studied briefly with Marcel Marceau, began his career by holding up the mime's mirror to shoppers and brown bag lunchers in San Francisco's Union Square. He has moved on to perform his improvisational style of mime on national television with his wife, Lorene Yarnell.

When performance takes to the street, the barrier between performer and audience fades. Toad the Mime (Antoinette Attell), another street performer who has moved to television, is unexcelled at enticing members of her audience into her act. She has made good use of the special participatory quality of mime in her work with prisons, retirement homes, and with deaf and blind audiences.

Some street performers, such as the San Francisco Mime Troupe, El Teatro Campesino, and the Bread and Puppet Theatre, use mime techniques to convey political messages. Others, such as Dolphin (Joe McCord), use mime to raise environmental issues. A seemingly simple story can imply strong social criticism through carefully executed illusions. In each of these instances, what makes mime such a powerful resource is the special way in which mime creates a bond between performer and audience.

Marcel Marceau

The Mime Experience

The mime speaks a universal language based on shared experiences. We all eat, walk, laugh, despair. When a mime eats an illusory apple, we taste it with her. We inwardly respond to a gesture we've made ourselves many times. Almost involuntarily, we munch and swallow, if only in our imaginations. With our consent, the mime walks up mountains, across deserts, and along the ocean floor. And we, the 'observers', go with him! It's our bodies' memories that transform the stylized act of walking into the illusion of going somewhere.

When a mime sheds a tear over a lost love, we share the experience because we've shed the tear, too. The particular loves may change, but the feeling of loss draws our empathy each time. All of our experiences, from the mundane to the momentous, get stored in our memories. Our dreams, successes, and frustrations furnish the raw material for the mime's fantasy. The mime is all of us.

The mime is you. It doesn't matter if you have the lean, lithe physique of a dancer or have acquired a beer belly from watching Sunday afternoon football on TV. In mime, anybody (in any condition) can play. You don't need a stage, script, costumes, or props. All that's required is a healthy imagination. You can create mime any time, anywhere—while you're sitting in the bathtub or waiting for the bus.

You already know the basic language of mime. You've been using it for years. A shrug of your shoulder, a push of the air with your hands, a raise of your eyebrow, all clearly communicate your wishes and feelings. We're all experts at body language.

Start by experimenting with the mime's vocabulary. As you try some of the warm-ups and basic techniques, you'll find your body becoming more responsive to your imagination. What you visualize your body doing is what it does. With concentration, practice, and patience you'll be able to juggle, walk a tightrope, become a hero or a villain (or both!). Your sense of accomplishment will remain long after your illusion has vanished.

Remember your childhood fantasy of rubbing a magic lamp and producing a genie who would grant you three wishes? In mime you're both the lamp holder and the genie.

Your wish is *your* command. You can create your own reality, extend your physical powers, and explore your emotions. Because you're talking with movement and gesture, you may find yourself 'saying' things you would never commit to words. If

your fantasy life seems to have atrophied over the years, that's all the more reason to create that magic lamp and start polishing.

Mime as Play

To become a professional mime requires a major commitment to the art. Performing mimes devote years of their lives to the perfection of their silent craft. They must master the traditional techniques and then give them new vitality with innovation and creativity. The learning and practicing never stops.

But you don't have to aspire to be a performer to enjoy being a mime. You can create mime in the spirit of play—not play as in 'theater', but play as in a game. Just as you played 'cops and robbers' or 'house', you can play at mime to create your own world and amuse yourself within it. It doesn't matter if you don't think of yourself as artistic or graceful—no one's keeping score in this game. If you let yourself be guided by imagination and really *feel* your fantasy, your illusion, with all its art and grace, will naturally follow.

As with any game, mime is more fun when it's shared with a friend. In mime play, when you add another player, you add another imagination, more energy, and a whole new collection of fantasies. Working together to maintain a mutual fantasy becomes a game in itself. You have to remain aware of each other's illusions or you'll walk right through them! As you improvise your scenario, you'll realize how important it is to communicate clearly. (What happens when you hand an illusory hammer to your partner and she uses it to take a drink?) Working with a partner to create illusions such as puppet and

Playing with this Book

This book is not designed to be a course in mime. Rather, it's an invitation for you to explore your body and your imagination. The warm-ups, exercises, games, and routines that follow are offered as a way of enriching your mime vocabulary and giving you an opportunity to play.

Each section of the book contains presentations of specific techniques followed by games that can be played with partners or groups. At the end of each chapter are some suggested 'routines'. You don't have to start at the beginning and work straight through; you can skim and play with whatever catches your imagination. If you'd prefer to follow a lesson-by-lesson progression, or want to present mime to a class or group, you can follow the Lesson Plan in the Appendix.

Above all, don't think of any of the games in the book as pieces to be 'performed'. Use them as jumping-off places—suggestions to spark your own improvisation and creativity. And remember, it is *your* imagination that makes the illusions on these pages become real.

You want to be a mime? You are! Discover the mime inside you and start to play.

puppeteer or mirror images becomes a study in observation, imitation, and rapport.

When you add more people to mime play, cooperation becomes the key. It doesn't matter who wins the tug-of-war—there's no trophy. (There's not even a rope!) Following the movements of your team members as they haul back and forth is the real challenge. Since you're creating the game, you can make up the rules so that everyone can play. When you enact a scene

from the Old West, you can have players ride horses, sit and play poker, pour drinks, play music, and end with a rousing brawl. Any self-consciousness you may have felt in creating your fantasies will disappear as you all contribute to making the moment alive with illusion.

Finally, should you decide that the game that really challenges you is performance, try entering it in the spirit of play. Remember that in mime your audience is always part of the game. Your spectators are your partners. They create your illusions with you. When you've managed to make your fantasy *their* fantasy, you've communicated.

ONE

Warm-ups

Anything you do throughout the day can be a warm-up for mime. When you're taking a shower, feel the water on your back, the smooth soap in your hand, the resistance of the faucet as you turn it on and off, the rough towel on your skin. Perhaps your shower lasts fifteen minutes. You can mime the experience in fifteen seconds—a turn of the faucet, a few wiggles beneath the water and the towel, and you're clean. You've recreated the shower for yourself and anyone watching.

Creating this illusion takes careful observation and body memory. When you tense your hand muscles around a faucet, really feel it. With the memory of that shape, you can tense your muscles around thin air, twist, and water will shower down.

In mime each movement must be clear enough to command attention. If the observer misses a key movement of a routine, it's like losing the third clue in a treasure hunt. You can't say in words, "Watch my hands because I'm going to turn on a water faucet to take a shower." And if that key action is missed, you'll look like you're being tickled instead of showered. In recreating an action, select the essential details, use the minimum of movements to convey them, and make each one count.

To emphasize the beginning and end of a movement, the mime uses the 'snap'—an exaggerated stop and start. The snap can be made with your hands, your eyes, your chest—your whole body. Sometimes it's big, sometimes it's almost imperceptible, but it's there. Although at first you'll have to remember to use the snap, with practice it will become natural to your mime movements.

Learning how to 'do nothing' with your body is another important part of mime. It's like neutral in a stick-shift car—you always return to it before shifting into a new gear. Neutral in mime is a chance to compose yourself, to pull all your energies together and focus on what you're going to say. You don't need a curtain going up to begin a routine—just snap from neutral into action. When you return to neutral, you've dropped your own illusory curtain, and it's clear that your communication is complete.

Your body and imagination are your tools in mime. The following exercises are intended to warm up both. They illustrate the basic principles of mime—to observe and imitate, to isolate and focus, to use your body memory. You don't have to think about how you will be using them. Just enjoy the doing.

Silence

Big X

Lie on your back.
Stretch your arms and legs out, making a big X with your body.

Press your body into the floor.
Press with your heels, your legs and arms, your spine, the back of your head. Try to make a dent in the floor by pushing down as hard as you can! Hold, then relax.

Let your body float up toward the ceiling.
Imagine that your nose, stomach, knees, and toes graze the ceiling as you hover there. Hold the position (ever so lightly). Then relax.

Tense and relax each part of your body.
Starting at your feet, stretch your toes, tense them, hold, and relax. Tense your right leg, hold, and relax. Continue up your body through your abdomen, chest, shoulders, arms, neck, face. Don't forget your fingers and even your tongue.

Breathe deeply,
filling your abdomen and chest. Hold. Exhale, listening to the sound of your breath. Take two more breaths and exhale, listening.

Take a deep breath silently.
Listen to the silence as you exhale. Repeat.

Consider what your body is like when it's silent.
Stay immobile and soundless. Feel the qualities of this state (inside and outside your body) so you can return to it as the basis for your neutral position.

Neutral

Stand with your feet shoulder width apart.
Distribute your weight equally on the heels and balls of your feet.

Bend your knees slightly to straighten your back.
Keep them relaxed, not locked.

Pull your buttocks under and in.
Tighten your stomach and abdomen.

Open your chest and shoulders,
then let them fall comfortably into place.

Let your head rest on the top of your spine,
not pushed forward or bent back. Your chin is parallel to the floor.

Relax your face.
Feel your jaw, mouth, forehead, and temples grow slack. Your eyes look straight ahead at nothing.

Think silence.
You are relaxed but alert and maintaining a precise posture. If you begin to smile or your weight starts to shift, bring yourself back to neutral.

Abruptly switch from neutral into jogging in place.
Abruptly return to neutral and mentally check your position and attitude. Make any corrections needed. Repeat until you can move easily and cleanly from neutral into action and back again.

Focus

Hands Up

Stand with your arms held out to your sides,
shoulder height. One by one, curl your fingers into your palm. Release by uncurling each finger individually. Repeat.

Clench your hands into tight fists.
Release, stretching your thumbs and fingers as far away from each other as you can.

Bring your palms together,
fingers pointing up, elbows held out. Press your palms together hard. Keeping your thumbs and fingertips touching, pull your palms away from each other in the direction of your elbows. Repeat the push and pull.

Extend your arms out in front of you,
palms parallel to the floor. Your fingers are straight and close together. Without bending your knuckles, snap your hands up. Point your fingertips back toward you as far as you can. Now snap your hands down, pointing your fingertips toward the floor. Keep your knuckles tight.

Undulate your hand,
curling your fingers in and out of your palm. Let your wrist lead the movement up and down, but keep your elbows fixed in place.

Marionette

Stand, bent over at the waist.
Your head hangs down, arms dangle loose, knees relax. You are a marionette, held up by strings.

Bounce up and down.
Imagine that an invisible puppeteer is tugging the string at the center of your back. Think string, not muscle.

Your back string pulls you up to standing position.
Your head string slowly pulls up until your face is forward and chin parallel to the floor. Your head settles in with a wobble.

Your head falls forward.
The head string pulls it in a circle, and then around again to the other side. (You are not *doing* the action but responding to the pull.)

One shoulder string pulls your shoulder up and forward.
Now back. Your arm remains limp. Now the other shoulder is rotated. Both shoulders together. Now in opposite directions.

One string pulls an elbow up,
to shoulder height. Your forearm dangles loosely. The wrist string lifts your forearm up and spins it like a windmill. The string lets loose and your arm falls. Zoomp! Up goes the other elbow and the windmill begins again.

Your wrist strings lift both arms out,
to the sides and up to shoulder height. Your hands rotate forward, pulled by the strings on the back of them. Faster. Suddenly all your arm strings let go. Flop!

One knee string pulls up and rotates your upper leg.
Your ankle string tugs forward to rotate your calf and foot. Then the string in the center of your foot lifts and rotates it. Slowly your imaginary puppeteer loosens your knee string until you are standing again on two feet. Whoops! There goes the other knee. . .

All strings on the right side pull up.
The other side slumps down. Now the left side strings are lifted.

You are lifted completely off the ground,
just for an instant. Then all the strings holding the top of your body let loose. Slump. You are as you began—a lifeless marionette.

Now try this exercise with a partner,
standing on a chair behind you and pulling on your strings. *You* are actually the one initiating the movement, and the puppeteer follows. Move slowly so your partner can move with you. Want to change places? A single twirl is enough to make the puppeteer gladly hand over those strings.

Magic Shoes

Pick up a pair of magic shoes.
Examine them curiously.

Put on one shoe.
Be sure you are sitting or in a well-balanced stance, because as soon as the shoe is laced and tied, your foot goes into *action!* It flutters, kicks, wiggles as if it had a life of its own. (The foot moves as if isolated from the rest of your body.)

Try to stop your frenetic foot by grabbing it.
Nice try—but now your hands are moving, too!

Remove the shoe.
Instantly your foot becomes still.

Put on both shoes.
Tap dance, jump, cavort! Take your magic shoes off. Rest.

Try on a magic hat, gloves, belt.
Each piece of magic clothing you put on energizes an isolated part of your body.

Snap

Robot

Stand straight and rigid.
You are a robot made up of solid units, connected at a few main joints.

Lift your forearm in a series of five jerks.
Snap into each movement, emphasizing the start and stop. Lower your arm in the same way.

Test all your body parts,
one by one. Turn your head and neck jerkily (like an android). Jerk your shoulders up and down. Turn at the waist in a series of jerks, and so on down your whole body. Only one part moves at a time, starting and stopping with precision.

Now gather together a group of robots,
and let a human press your buttons (without touching of course!). It works best for the buttons to be on the side or front so you can see what's happening.

Take a walk.
If you're on a collision course with another robot, snap into a different direction. If you hit a wall, move in place until your human turns you. If you fall down, keep your feet moving in the air until you're rescued.

Wind down.
Your movements gradually slow to a stop (a silent whirr . . .).

Pulling Punches

In slow motion, give your partner a right to the jaw. The 'hit' comes to a sudden halt about an inch from your victim's chin. Your swing follows through in slow motion. (Remember, body contact in mime is illusory.)

The partner responds to the hit with a snap of the head, and reels away from the blow in slow motion.

Exchange blows— to the jaw, midsection, legs— following the same sequence of hit, snap, and follow through. You can kick and slap as well—whatever suits your aggression!

Fall slowly,

breathing out as you go down, catching yourself with your hands before your body lands. Turn your head to avoid landing on your chin. A somersault is an easy follow through if you curl up as you go down.

Gather a group of combatants,

then have an all-out, slow-motion, no-touching brawl.

Image

Midnight Snack

With closed eyes, visualize a refrigerator,
stocked with your favorite munchies. Consider the shape, color and texture of each food. How might each one taste?

Open your eyes and open the refrigerator.
Take out everything you'll need to concoct a midnight snack.

Feel each food in your hand.
Is it bumpy or smooth? Soft or fuzzy? Peel, unwrap, slice, spread, or stir as necessary.

Take a bite; have a slurp.
Is it just what you imagined?

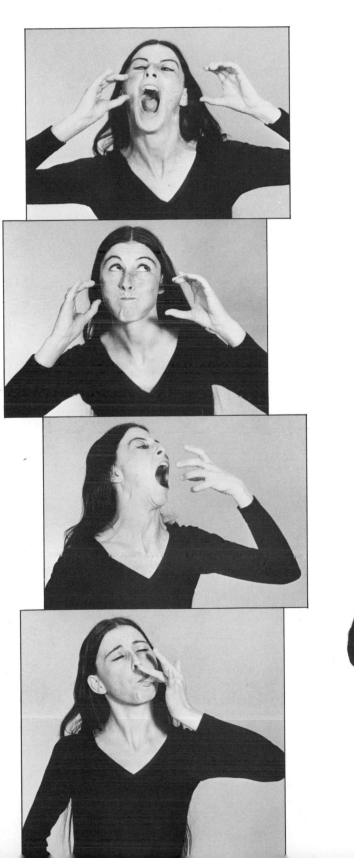

Mirror

You and your partner are mirror images.
Stand facing each other with at least a foot of space between you.

One of you make a face.
The 'mirror' simultaneously makes the same face. Your expression changes to surprise—and so does the expression in the mirror, immediately and exactly. Keep changing your expressions, but slowly enough so the mirror can follow you.

Change roles and add simple body movements.
Start with the head and move through all parts of the body. Continue to move slowly.

Take turns being different characters—
an inquisitive child, a young boy admiring himself, a woman putting on makeup. There will be lots going on, so watch 'yourselves.'

Face Passing

Everyone sit in a circle,
facing the back of the person in front of you. (Focus on the back of their head, not beyond.) Your faces are in neutral.

One of you create a face.
Turn around and show it to the person behind and return to neutral. The movement is quick and precise.

The receiver imitates the face and passes it on.
The face continues around the circle until it reaches its original creator, who shows the group the ending face—and the starting face. With practice, the same face will make it all the way around.

For variation, everyone sit facing the center of the circle.
One of you make a face.

Throw the new face to someone else,
who receives it, changes it, and passes it on. Metamorphosis!

Flying Machine

Gather five people.
You are going to construct a flying machine.

Assign each person a specific part of the airplane.
One person can be the cockpit, two people each of the wings, and two people, with crossed hands, the propellers.

Assemble and take off.
Soar into the air. Bank around turns. Swoop into a nose dive. The key is to keep moving as a unit.

Stage an air show.
Ten people can form a huge transport; pairs can be swift aerobatic planes, flying in close formation. The only limit is your imagination.

The Frog

The Mime enters carrying a
small creature cupped in her
hands. She strokes it gently, smiling.
A chuck under the chin . . . oops.
Sproing! With her eyes, the Mime
follows the creature through the air
to the floor. *Umph.* Quick, before
someone steps on the little fellow.
She walks over to pick up the Frog.
Sproing . . . sproing . . . gotcha!
Nope. As hop becomes jump, the
Mime's head gets into the action.
Her neck and shoulders follow leap
and bound. Her back enters the act,
and soon her knees as well follow
the frog's wild cavorting. Her whole
body is jumping now. Where will it
all end? Oh no . . . the Mime's arms
drop between her bent legs. With a
suspiciously wide grin on her face,
she casually springs up to catch a
passing fly. *Gulp.* Silent croak of
pleasure.

T W O

Objects

In mime, you're a magician. With a little sleight of hand, you can make anything you want—a magic lamp complete with genie, a chocolate sundae, a whole house—and furnished too! Once you've visualized what you want and selected the details, your hands make the object tangible by giving it shape, weight, and texture. You're not really creating something new but recreating an illusion everyone knows.

Though we often 'talk with our hands', asking our hands to do *all* the talking requires some movements that at first seem unnatural. Bending your hands into 90-degree angles takes concentration and practice—we're more used to moving in curves. Approaching a ball with a flat hand seems artificial, but it allows you to clearly define the curved shape by contrast. When you set the ball aside, your hand snaps flat once again. If you don't define the moment of release, you've taken the ball with you! The value of contrast works the same way when you snap a relaxed hand flat to place your table exactly where you want it to be. Pausing after you create each object—if only for an instant—may take a conscious effort, but it allows you and your audience the time to register your illusion.

To be a good magician you have to make every action count. (Wriggle your finger while you're holding a baseball, and you'll transform it into a sponge ball.) Once you've created the object, tensing your hand helps you to remember the exact shape. You can leave it and return to the *same* object with ease.

The following exercises offer the 'basic vocabulary' of creating objects. Once you've learned the language, you can go from there to do whatever you want. One shape can become anything else. A wall can become a door . . . can become a window . . . can become a house. Just keep in mind that as a mime magician your intention is not to deceive but to communicate. Present your objects clearly and simply. Mime is not a guessing game. And once you've created your objects, remember where you've put them. (Your audience will.) If you forget, you'll end up tripping over your illusions with your hands full!

Balls

Creating a Ball

Visualize a volleyball,
suspended in space before you.

**Approach the ball with a
flat hand,**
allowing your entire arm to make the movement. As you connect with the surface of the ball, your hand snaps into a curve. Discover the shape in your palm as well as with your fingers.

**Snap your other hand from
flat to curved,**
on the opposite side of the ball. The curves mirror each other exactly. Tense your hands to maintain the shape you have created.

792152

CICERO PUBLIC LIBRARY

Exploring a Ball

Explore the shape of the ball.
Hold it by the sides, by the top and
bottom. Balance it in one hand. Lift
your elbows away from your body
and let your arms move with the
ball.

Feel the texture of the ball.
Slide your fingers over its smooth
surface. Change the texture. Ripple
your fingers over the bumpy surface
of a basketball. Squeeze a spongy
ball.

Feel the weight of the ball.
Make it light. Make it heavy. You can
feel the strain in your arms, bended
knees, and back as you lift a heavy
ball above your head. Silent groan!

Tossing a Ball

Create a ball you can hold in one hand.
Your palm and fingers outline its shape. Steady your focus on the ball.

Toss the ball into the air.
Your hand snaps flat as the ball leaves your palm.

Follow its ascent and descent with your eyes and head.
Your waiting palm is stretched flat.

Emphasize the catch.
When the ball lands in your hand, simultaneously 1) your palm and fingers snap into the curve of the ball, 2) your hand snaps slightly downward with the weight, 3) your head snaps and stops abruptly as the ball comes to rest. The lighter the ball, the subtler these movements will be, but even a featherweight ping-pong ball gets the snap treatment.

Repeat tossing and catching many kinds of balls,
using one hand or both hands. Try billiard balls, balloons, Earthballs, and marbles.

Ball Games

Toss a ball to another person.
Your eyes and head show where it's going. Both players' heads snap to emphasize the catch.

Roll the ball to another person.
Let your whole body glide to describe the rolling. Emphasize the catch with a snap and a hold.

Bounce a ball to another person.
Together, follow the bounce with your head and eyes. Your heads snap simultaneously on the catch.

Gather a team for some ball games.
Visualize a net and play tennis or volleyball. Shoot baskets. Hit home runs. Line up at scrimmage and try a slow motion forward pass. To keep all eyes on one ball is really the game here.

Tables

Creating a Table Top

Visualize a table before you, waist high.

Approach the table top with a relaxed hand.
As your hand contacts the surface, it snaps flat and stops abruptly. Feel the moment of contact with your whole body. Tense your hand to hold it flat. Feel the tension up to your shoulder.

Remove your hand from the table and repeat.
Snap flat, tense, hold. Is your table still waist high? Repeat until you can consistently return to the same level with a flat hand.

Hitting a Table

Move your hand slowly across a table top.
Maintain the tension in your arm. Move your hand in a circle over the surface. Rub the surface gently, then really polish it.

Slap the table top.
Lift your hand, relax it, and slap the table again. Tense and hold at each slap to maintain the illusion of the surface.

Make a fist and pound the table.
Maintain the tension with your whole arm. Lift your fist above your head and slam it back down on the table. Try using your whole body to express the abrupt contact. Tense your arm and shoulder, neck, and back. Even your legs feel the impact. Be careful to keep your fist from crashing through the table!

Moving Tables

Place your hand on a table waist high.
Snap flat, tense. Move your hand across the top.

Grip the sides of the table,
fingers bent at the knuckle to form a 90-degree angle. Tilt! You can't lift it alone.

Have your partner grip the opposite side,
carefully following the dimensions you have set for the table. Both of you tense your arms all the way to the shoulder to maintain the size of the table.

Together, lift the table.
Maintaining your grip, lift your shoulders and arms as a unit. With practice, you'll smooth out that wavy table!

Walk a few steps together and put the table down.
Maintaining your grip, lower your shoulders and arms. Release your hands. Is the table still waist high?

Both of you place an elbow on the table.
Indian wrestle? Clasp hands. Go! Don't forget to keep your elbows on, not through, the same table top.

Walls

Creating a Wall

Visualize a wall.
Notice exactly how close it is to you.

Approach the wall with a relaxed hand.
When you meet it, your hand snaps flat, stops abruptly, and your muscles tense to hold the position.

Lift your other hand to meet the wall.
Snap flat, tense, and hold. Slide your hands toward each other across the wall. Are both hands on the same plane?

Keep one hand on the wall and lift the other.
Relax it and touch the wall in a different place. Snap flat, tense, and hold.

Continue to explore your wall, lifting and replacing one hand at a time. Move your hands up, down, sideways, around. Keeping both hands in view will help maintain the same plane.

Follow your wall down to the floor.
Leading with the heel of your hands, slide them toward the floor. Your fingers are pulled back flat, the tension in your whole body maintains the position of your hands. As you move below your waist level, turn your hands and point your fingers downward.

Follow your wall to the corner on your right.
Lift your right hand, relax it, and place it on the adjoining wall. Notice the corner where your two walls meet. Slide your left hand to the corner, snap-turn it onto the other wall, and keep sliding until your hands meet. Don't forget to take your body along with you!

Looking Over a Wall

Create a wall.
Slide your hands up the wall until they reach eye level. Stop.

Snap your fingers forward,
perpendicular to your palm. Tense your arms and hold. Your face expresses your curiosity.

Raise up on your toes,
keeping your hands in place. You move—the wall is stationary.

Peer over the wall.
Your face snaps into surprise at the precise moment you can see over the wall. This change of expression enhances the illusion of a solid wall. Lower yourself down, keeping your hands in place.

Repeat using different expressions.

Making an Opening

Create a wall with a partner, one of you on either side.
Together, discover its width and height. Avoid looking directly at each other—remember, there's a solid wall between you.

Knock on the wall.
Your partner hears and moves toward the sound, listening. Your partner knocks back. Bob your head in rhythm as you hear the knocks. Move around the wall, knocking, pounding, scratching. Listen and respond to each other.

Make an opening in the wall.
Dig out a hole, undo a loose plank, or pull out a brick. Reach through the opening.

Look through the opening.
You see each other. Both begin expanding the opening until it is big enough for one to crawl through.

Both of you place your hands on the same side of the wall.
Maintain the plane established by the person on the right. Move along the wall together, lifting and placing your hands precisely.

Pushing Over a Wall

Place your hands on a wall.
Keeping them tensed and in position, push your torso away, moving through your shoulders. The wall doesn't budge.

Try again, this time moving your hands slowly and steadily forward.
Your body follows. Your chest leads the effort. Feel the tension in your arching back.

Slowly tilt your hands,
maintaining the same plane. Stop. Move your body slightly away from the wall, pausing an instant before the final thrust. Feeling the effort with your whole body, give a last push. Success!

Follow the falling wall with your eyes and head.
Your head nods to emphasize the crash. Hold your focus while the dust settles.

...ust be careful the wall
...oesn't fall over on you!

Boxes

Visualize a box,
suspended in space before you. It is
about a foot square.

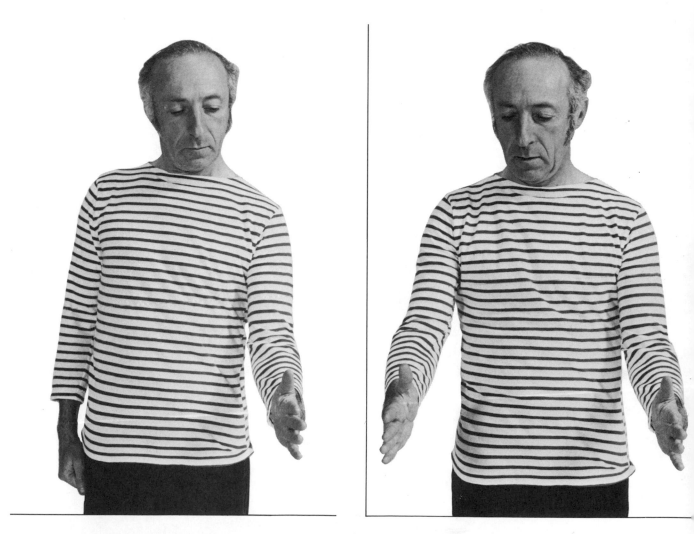

pproach the box with a elaxed hand,

sing your entire arm to make the novement. When you connect with he side of the box, your hand snaps at, head snaps forward slightly. ense your hand and arm to naintain the position.

Lift your other hand and place it on the opposite side of the box.

Snap, tense, and hold. You have established the width of your box.

Lift one hand and place it on the bottom of the box.

Snap, tense, and hold. Place the other hand on top of the box. Your box now has height.

Lifting a Box

Visualize a box on the floor.
Bend over and place your hands on top of it. Snap flat, tense, and hold. Place your hands on each side.

Lift a light box.
Experience the lifting with your back, shoulders, and arms. Return the box to the floor. Emphasize the moment of contact with a slight snap of your head.

Lift a heavy box.
Slip your fingers under either side of the box, bending them at the knuckle to create a 90-degree angle Tense and hold. Keeping your fingers in touch with the floor, first bend your knees and elbows, then straighten them abruptly. Repeat. The box won't move!

Try again,
this time with success. As you lift the box, feel its weight in your bent knees, in your back and shoulders, in your straining neck muscles. Slowly straighten your knees as you raise the box to waist level. Stagger away with it.

Opening a Box

Create a large box on the floor.
Kneel down in front of it.

Bend your fingers at the knuckle to form an angle to lift the cover.
It sticks. Relax one hand and place it on another edge of the lid, knuckles bent. Pry up. Continue to loosen the edges until the lid lifts. Maintaining its angles as you move it, place the lid on the floor.

Peer into the box.
Curiosity. Surprise. Reach in and lift out a smaller box. Place it on the floor. (Remember where you left the lid!) This box has a hinged lid.

With flat hands parallel to the sides of the box, extend your thumbs at a 90-degree angle.
Lifting your arms from the shoulder, tilt your hands as the lid lifts. Peek inside. Bring the lid down abruptly. Slam! It's not what you had hoped for.

Lift the lid again,
one hand on the side of the box, the other lifting with fingertips. Your arm creates a broad arc as the lid rises.

Reach inside and remove another box.
Repeat ad infinitum . . . or until you need a magnifying glass.

Movers

Create a very big box and try to push it.
Snap your hands flat against the side of the box, tense, and hold. Keeping your hands in place, straighten your elbows, pushing your shoulders and chest away from the box. Oof! It won't budge.

Push with your shoulder.
Place your arm from shoulder to elbow flat against the box. As your arm and torso move toward the box, your hips move away from it. Ungh! Still no luck.

Push with your bottom.
Start with your pelvis shifted forward, buttocks tucked under. As you push, arch your back and pelvis back toward the box, and push your chest forward and up. The box still won't move! Call (silently) for some others to help.

Everyone push against the box.
Use different parts of your bodies, watching each other to maintain the shape of the box. All together, one . . . two . . . three . . . puuuush! The box begins to move slowly, as do all of you together.

**Everyone form a chain
and pass boxes.**
With palms extended flat, bob your
hands down as you receive the box.
Follow the cue of the person passing
it. Does their body say 'small but
heavy'? 'Small and light'?

**Stack several small boxes
on one hand.**
As you add each box to the top of
the stack, drop your bottom hand an
equal distance down. Pass the stack
on to someone else who adds to
it—too many boxes. Crash!

Shapes

Visualize before you a pile of assorted junk—
balls, boxes, bottles, cups, tubes, blankets, etc. You have with you a big empty sack for your collection.

Discover a ball.
Pick it up. Toss it in the air and bounce it a few times. Toss it up and catch it in your sack.

Pick up a small box.
Turn the combination dial or pick the lock. Anything inside? Put the box in your sack.

Select a wide-mouthed jar with a lid.
Tense your hand around the lid to maintain its shape as you turn it counterclockwise, moving from the wrist. Pheeew! What an odor. Screw the lid back on clockwise. Toss it away.

Pick up a bottle.
It still has liquid in it. Pry off the cork. Select a glass from the pile, blow out the dust (cough), and pour. Indicate the filling of the glass by lowering it slightly. Finish pouring with a snap. Drink. (Hic!)

Pull out a soggy blanket.
Grasp it a section at a time and twist your hands in opposite directions to wring it out. The blanket should feel a lot lighter when you're done. Fold it and drop it into your sack.

Continue your treasure hunt,
until your sack is bulging full, then carry or drag it away.

Changing Shapes

Create a beachball.
With great effort, gradually squeeeeze it to the size of a baseball. Feel the change of size and shape with your whole hand. Your entire body feels the exertion. Your face expresses it, too.

Strrrretch the baseball into a long cylinder.
Tense and hold to maintain the two ends of the cylinder.

Roll the cylinder between your hands,
narrowing it into a long noodle. Twirl the noodle. Wiggle it.

Gather the noodle into a mass.
Smooth it into a flat disk. Roll it. Sail it like a Frisbee.

Fold the disk in half,
in half again, and so on until it is a speck in the palm of your hand. Blow it away.

Repeat the above changes,
making them in a series of abrupt exertions. Exaggerate the start and stop of each exertion. It may take three stages to get from beachball to baseball.

Gifts

With a group of friends, create a large box.
Stand around it in a circle.

One of you open the box, and take out an object. Define it with your hands. Use it. Give it to someone else in the circle.

The receiver stretches or squashes or pulls the gift into the shape of another object.
A telescope can become a cane, a cane a trombone; a trombone can stretch into an accordian.

In turn, each person passes the transformed gift on to someone else.
If the receivers prefer, they can return the gift to the center box and take out a new object to use and pass on.

The Juggler

The Mime casually tosses a small ball into the air and catches it. Up . . . down . . . his head follows. Up . . . turn around . . . down. Kick it up with the toe . . . down, catch. Fancee! Grin. He reaches deep into a huge pocket and comes out with another ball. Toss up one and catch. Toss up the other and catch. Toss up both and . . . whoops. His head bobs in time with the balls as they bounce away. Blush. Deep into the pocket again, this time out with one more. One toss . . . two toss . . . pass . . . three toss . . . catch . . . pass . . .

toss . . . catch-pass-toss catch-pass-toss. . . . His head traces their easy circling. He catches the balls, pocket them and bows. Honest pride. The Mime peers at the audience.

They want four? Into the pocket again. With panache, four balls are sent aloft. Bow. Five? Six? Seven? What's the limit? With a wink, the Mime produces ten balls. He starts them into orbit. Frenetic whirring. His hands become a blur. Ten balls! Somehow, he manages a full-scale bow while the balls are still busy circling. Ta dum! Still juggling, he takes another bow . . . and another . . . until . . . he looks up, and becomes lost in a shower of cascading spheres. An encore?

THREE

Movements

You are about to defy all laws of gravity as you go up and down invisible ladders, steps, and ropes. Supported by levitation? No—imagination! When a mime flies overhead on a magic carpet, the mime and the audience have made a pact about reality—they've agreed to share an illusion. Anything is possible—if *you* are convinced and comfortable with your movements.

With one movement you can create a whole environment—the wild west as you ride your bronco, a ship at sea as you sway at the railing. Using the illusory walk, you can go miles standing in a twelve-inch circle. When you turn your back and walk 'away', slowing to a stop, the audience knows you have faded from sight, even though you're still there! You can climb a ladder with your feet on the floor—looking *down* at the scene below you puts you *up* by contrast.

At first these stylized movements will feel unnatural to you—sort of like patting your head while rubbing your stomach. With practice, the movements will become rhythmic and automatic, and your audience will see them as natural. The focus will be on your story rather than your technique. The experience you elicit will be "She's walking on the moon," not "What a great fake walk in an imaginary place."

Some of the following exercises give instructions for hands and feet or arms and legs. Practice them separately at first. When you feel comfortable with the rhythm of each, combine them, slowly at first. Gradually increase your speed, as you focus on how your total body is creating the movement.

Once you've practiced these basic movements, you'll be able to perfect more complex ones. Start by analyzing how each part of the body should respond—head, shoulder, arms, hips, legs. You'll discover that as one part of the body acts, another part reacts, often in the opposite direction. (Newton's Third Law of Motion applies to mimes too.) Keeping this principle in mind will give your movements emphasis and realism.

As with all the exercises in this book, try to practice them with your friends—make games out of them. A stationary trek across an illusory desert is much more bearable with a companion.

Walking

Easy Walk

Stand in neutral with your feet about nine inches apart, your weight on the balls of your feet. Only your heels will move in this walk.

Raise your right heel, bending your right knee. Feel the shift in your pelvis as your right hip moves forward too. The ball of your foot remains stationary, as if glued to the floor.

As you lower your right heel, raise your left heel. Do this simultaneously. Don't wait for your right heel to settle before moving your left.

Repeat, lowering your left heel, raising your right. Again, feel the movement in your hips. All the action is taking place from your waist down. Your head remains level, not bobbing up and down. Direct the movement in your knees forward rather than upward. Both knees remain flexed, not locked tight, and your toes are firmly in place.

Let your arms swing naturally with the movement. Usually the left arm moves forward with the right knee and vice versa.

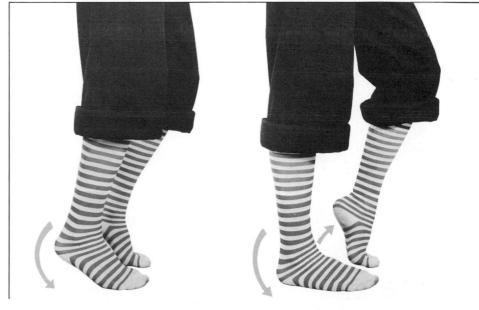

Sliding Walk

Begin in neutral, facing your audience.

Bend your right knee forward, lifting your right heel. Shift your weight to the ball of your right foot.

Straighten your right knee, lowering your right heel. As your right heel touches the floor, slide your left foot out behind you (as if wiping something off your shoe).

Bring your left foot around and forward in a small arc, back to its starting place. Land on the ball of your left foot.

Shift your weight to your left foot, straightening your left knee. As your left heel touches, slide your right foot back, as you did with the left.

Repeat, alternating legs,
until the rhythm is smooth. Feel the
movement in your hips and knees.

**Keep your head and
torso level.**
Let your arms swing naturally, usually
left arm forward as the right knee
goes forward and vice versa.

Profile Walk

Begin in neutral,
your side to the audience.

Shift your weight to your left foot.
Holding your right foot flexed, extend it forward. Your right knee remains straight.

Sliding your right foot back into place,
bend your left knee, lift your left heel and roll your weight onto the ball of your left foot. The sliding of your right foot and lifting of your left heel happen simultaneously.

Shift your weight to your right foot.
Extend your left foot forward, knee straight.

Sliding your left foot back into place,
bend your right knee, lift your right heel. Shift your weight onto the ball of your left foot, releasing your right for another step.

Repeat the movement until it is smooth.
Slide and lift, then shift. Keeping head and torso level, feel the action in your pelvis and legs.

Let your arms follow the movement naturally.

Follow the Leader

Stand where you can see the leader.
Give yourselves sufficient space to do the mime walk freely.

Follow the leader as he walks through a series of environments.
The leader chooses any of the illusory walks (easy, sliding, profile) or switches from one to another during the journey. He may change the pace from slow to fast to running. You are led through rain, mud, fog, over puddles, through snow drifts, across desert sands, up a dune, into the wind.

Switch leaders.
Move through more abstract environments such as feathers, honey, peanut butter, cobwebs, outer space—anything goes! Wherever your journey takes you, you're sure to end up exactly where you started.

Climbing

Subway

You are about to descend the stairs into a subway station.
Wave farewell to your friends, and step behind a waist-high box or sheet of stiff free-standing material. Look down the stairs.

Step forward,
bend your knees slightly, and drop your whole body (no more than three inches at a time). Keep your back straight.

Step again and drop down a bit more.
Feel those thigh muscles working. Continue stepping and bending until you are crouched down and completely hidden behind the prop.

Turn around,
remaining crouched. Take a step forward, coming up three inches, back straight. Continue until you are back on the street again.

Rush hour!
Several people are going down the subway steps as others are coming up. Greet each other as you pass.

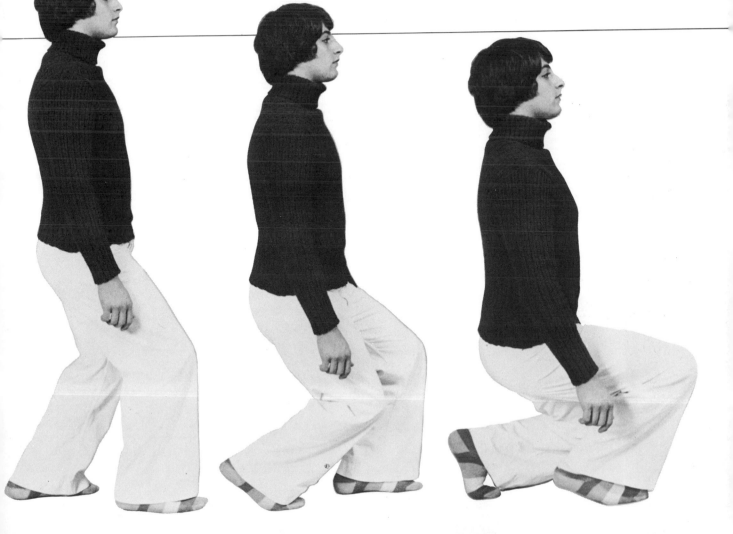

Up Stairs

Practice the instructions for hands and feet separately; then combine, slowly at first.

HANDS

Look up at an imaginary bannister,

on your right. Lean slightly forward and extend your arm with a relaxed hand. Grasp the bannister at shoulder height. Tense your hand to maintain the shape.

Pull your hand diagonally down to your waist,

as if you were sliding your hand down the bannister. The illusion is that your hand remains stationary while *you* move up the stairs.

Straighten your back,

while you continue sliding your hand down the bannister. Stop at hip level.

Reach forward and grasp the bannister again.

FEET

Stand with your feet together

Lift your right foot and place it slightly forward and up six inches onto the first step.

Step down onto the ball of your right foot.

Simultaneously come up onto the ball of your left foot. Both knees are now straight, weight equally distributed. (You will move slightly forward with each step.)

Come down on your right heel,

shifting your weight to your right foot. Your left heel remains up and your left knee bends.

Lift your left foot,

forward and up six inches onto the next step.

Down Stairs

Practice hands and feet separately; then combine.

HANDS

Look down at an imaginary bannister,

on your left. Lean back slightly and reach forward with a relaxed hand. Grasp the bannister at thigh level. Tense your hand to maintain the shape.

Pull your hand up toward you,

as though you were sliding your hand up the bannister. Stop at waist level.

Reach forward and grasp the bannister again.

You're ready to go down another step. Level your eyes when you get to the bottom.

FEET

Stand with your feet together.

Come up onto the ball of your right foot as you extend your straight left leg slightly forward over the imaginary step.

Bend your right knee.

Keeping your left leg straight, step down onto your left foot. (You will move slightly forward with each step.)

Come up onto the ball of your left foot,

as you extend your straight right leg slightly forward. You're ready to go down another step.

Up a Ladder

Practice hands and feet separately; then combine.

HANDS

Curl your hands around the ladder rungs.
Your right hand is at chin level, your left hand nine inches directly above it.

Bring both curled hands straight down,
maintaining the nine inch space between the rungs. Stop when the upper hand reaches chin level. Your eyes follow your hands down.

Lift your right hand,
now on the bottom rung. Look up and reach for the next rung.

Curl your hands around the ladder rungs.
Your left hand is now at chin level, your right hand nine inches directly above it.

Continue.
Bring both hands down, maintaining the space between them. Lift your left hand up to the next rung, and so on.

FEET

Stand with your feet together.
Lift your right foot up nine inches, and place the ball of your foot on the ladder rung.

Step straight down on the ball of your right foot,
as you simultaneously come up onto the ball of your left foot. Feel the exertion of lifting your body up the ladder. You are now standing on the balls of both feet with your knees straight.

Bend your left knee,
come down on your right heel, and straighten your right leg.

Lift your left foot nine inches up onto the next rung.

Continue.
Step down on the ball of your left foot, up on the ball of your right foot, knees straight. Bend your right knee, down on your left heel. Lift your right foot, and so on.

Down a Ladder

Practice hands and feet separately; then combine.

HANDS

Grasp the sides of the ladder.
Your hands are at shoulder level.

**Slide your hands up
nine inches,**
the equivalent of one rung, and
pause.

Hold your hands in place,
while you extend your leg.

**Slide your hands up another
nine inches,**
and pause.

**Lift your hands from the sides
of the ladder,**
one at a time, and place them as
they were, at shoulder level.
Continue.

FEET

Stand with both feet flat.
Bend your right leg and extend it
behind you.

**Come up on the ball of your
left foot.**
Simultaneously straighten your right
leg and bring it back into place, with
foot flat and leg straight.

**Bend your left leg and extend
it behind you.**

**Come up on the ball of your
right foot.**
Simultaneously straighten your left
leg and bring it back into place, with
foot flat and leg straight.

Hold this position,
while you lower your hands.
Continue.

Up a Rope

Practice arms and legs separately; then combine.

ARMS

Stretch your hands above your head.
Look up at the rope. Grasp the rope with your right hand above your left. (Leave room in your grip for the rope!) Tense your hands and arms in position and hold.

Pull your body up the rope,
sliding both hands straight down toward your chest. The muscles of your arms and back tense with the effort.

Stop and hold your hands in position at chest level.
Your knees get a new grip.

Reach up with your left hand.
Grasp the rope again. Follow with your right hand above it. You're ready to pull again.

LEGS

Stand cross-legged.
You are holding the rope between your knees.

Release the rope,
opening your knees out to the side. Lift up onto the balls of your feet.

Grab the rope between your knees.
Simultaneously lower your heels back to the floor.

Lock your knees around the rope and hold.
Let your hands get a new grip. You're ready to pull yourself up again.

Down a Rope

Practice arms and legs separately; then combine.

ARMS

Grasp the rope at chest level,
right hand above the left. Look down to where you're going.

Let your body down the rope,
sliding both hands up until they are stretched above you almost at arms' length.

Release your hands one at a time
and get a new grip on the rope back at chest level. You're ready to slide down again.

LEGS

Stand cross-legged,
holding the rope tight between your knees.

Open your knees out to the side,
releasing the rope between them.

Grab the rope quickly between your knees.
You're cross-legged again. Hold while your hands shift position. You're ready to slide down again.

Hang on!
It's a long way down.

Pulling

Rowing

Sit down,
knees slightly bent before you.

Grasp the handles of the oars in front of you,
chest high. Bend forward and push your hands away from you at waist level. There is little resistance in this movement.

Now pull!
Bring your hands up slightly and pull them toward your chest. Feel how much effort it takes to pull the oars through the water.

Repeat the rowing cycle.
Think *easy . . . haaard . . . easy . . . haaard . . .* giving the second portion a longer time. Feel the rhythm.

Row across the floor.
(Remember, you'll be moving backwards.) On 'easy', lean forward, bend your knees slightly and pull your feet closer toward you. On 'hard', lean back, dig in your heels and slide back on your rear end. (Doing this on a smooth floor is easier than on a rug!)

Get a sculling partner.
Step down into your racing shell. The boat rocks, then wobbles, finally balances. Sit. The second person's feet are alongside the person in front. The bow rower sets the pace for rowing and moving backwards.

Rope Pull

Visualize a thick rope,
suspended waist high before you. Stand facing it with your feet shoulder width apart.

Grab the rope,
reaching to your right with your right hand in front of your left. Tense your hands to maintain the shape.

Pull the rope toward you.
Think of your body in two pieces. First your torso leans forward and your hips jut back. As you bring your hands back to your chest (puuuulling), your torso leans back and your hips push forward. Let your knees bend and straighten naturally with the movement.

Get a new grip.
Release your left hand and reach in front of your right to grab the rope again. Release your right hand and place it in front of the left. Your torso is pushed forward again, your hips back. Pull!

Add a snap of your head.
As your hands reach forward, your head bends forward. When your hands reach your chest, snap your head back.

Tug of War

Two teams line up facing each other.
Watch carefully to see that you're all holding the same size rope.

On your mark!
Everyone dig in, straightening one leg, bending the other. Set your jaws and . . .

Pull!
Follow the movements of the person in front of you. Only your team captains will know for sure which side is pulling or being pulled, winning or losing. (This takes some real cooperation.)

One team begins to haul rope.
(Yea!) A few tough souls on the
other side get taken along. A few fall
as the rope slips their grip. It doesn't
matter who wins—the real game is
the illusion of pulling together.

Riding

Bicycle

Begin in neutral,

your right side to the audience. Your left foot will remain stationary throughout to balance your weight while your right leg does the pedaling.

Shift your weight onto your left leg,

bending slightly at the knee as you take a seat. Bend forward and grasp the handlebars. Keep your hands tensed in this position throughout.

Lift your right knee high,

toes pointed down. Push your chest forward. Begin a circular movement, bringing your right foot down parallel to the floor. Your left knee bends deeper.

Slide your right foot past its starting place,

back behind your body. Lift your knee again to complete the circle. As your knee lifts, point your toes again and slightly straighten your torso and left knee.

Repeat the circular pedaling movement,

keeping your hands tensed and steady on the handlebars. Bend left leg, lift right and circle, straighten left . . . Feel the rhythm up, down, and around.

Go tandem!

The rider on the back follows the movements of the person in front. Keep your handlebars at the same level. A word of warning: Riding a bicycle with one leg can be harder than riding a unicycle with two.

Horse

Stand with your back straight, feet shoulder width apart.

Bend both knees out to the side, and slowly lower down. Keep your back straight and rear end tucked under. 'Sit' as low as you can.

Grasp the reins, and you're ready to ride. As you ride, keep your head level and all the 'galloping' below the waist.

Lift your left heel. Rolling your weight along the outside of your foot, drop your heel. Lift your right heel and roll back. Continue. As you pick up speed, put a little snap into the rhythm.

Whoa! Pull back on the reins and dismount, swinging your leg up and over the horse. As your right foot hits the floor, dip down a bit. You're off—but your legs just won't straighten! Bowlegged, you walk off, swaying from side to side.

Ship Ahoy

Stand with your friends facing a ship railing.
Your feet are shoulder width apart.

Reach your arms straight out and grab the railing.
(Whoever touches the railing first establishes its height and size. Look at the hands of the person on your right to make sure you're holding the same railing throughout.) If your arms are longer than your mates', keep your elbows straight and move back. The ship begins to roll.

Roll with the waves!
Keeping your hands and feet in place, sway to the left, bending your left knee and straightening your right. Return to center. Now sway to the right, bending your right knee and straightening your left.

Keep your hands and feet stationary throughout.
Although the railing on a real ship would move diagonally with the rise and fall of the waves, keeping your hands parallel and in one place as your body sways makes the illusion work (mimetic license!).

Daedalus
and Icarus

Daedalus and his son Icarus are trapped in the labyrinth, prey to the Minotaur. Side by side, father and son move through the maze, their hands sliding along myriad walls, following endless corners. There is no way out. Gazing up, Daedalus sees a bird in flight. A feather drifts down. Freedom! Father and son begin gathering feathers and fashioning wings. Icarus slips into his wings, tests them, rises a few inches off the ground, and discovers that he *can* fly. Impatiently, Icarus rejoins his father, who is still binding his wings to his arms. Daedalus looks ahead to the sun, then cautiously extends his wings. With outstretched arms, father and son begin to fly—slowly, fluidly. They leave the labyrinth below; above them, the sun. They begin to feel the sun's heat melting the wax holding their wings. Daedalus draws back, but Icarus is enraptured with the power of flight. Daedalus' pleas go unheeded as Icarus soars towards the sun. Ascension. Pain. His wings disintegrate. Icarus spirals to earth.

F O U R

Characters

You can populate your mime world with as many characters as you can imagine. Now that you know how to create an illusory wall, you can push it over either as yourself— or as the Big Bad Wolf. You know how to walk up an invisible stairway, but doing it as an eighty-year-old grandfather or as a super-hero are entirely different experiences. Just decide who you want to be, feel it inside yourself, then choose the right movements and mannerisms to reveal your character.

Your body language says who your character is and what kind of world he or she lives in. With aggressive and purposeful gestures, chest thrust forward and body commanding space, you're confident. Or you can be cowardly with hesitant movements and caved-in chest. With the rhythm of your movement, you can express your character's age and attitude— the uncertainty of infancy, the abandon of youth, the caution of old age. You don't need words to say, "I'm sad, I may cry." When your face and body express only sadness everyone can recognize the emotion from their own experience.

You can be one character, then turn around, change your face and body, and come back as a different one. Don't limit yourself to humans—be Miss Muffet *and* the Spider! Be a camel or a whale. Be an object—a pinball machine, an apple, a mailbox.

The tools you have used in creating illusory objects and movements—the snap, focus, the ability to select and emphasize detail—help to create your character. Use them to clarify the quirks and habits that make your character unique. By adding a simple prop, you can further reveal who you are.

Watch people and animals, carefully observe objects, and keep a mental notebook. For your first character, try something obvious, like the basic villain. Ask yourself, "As a villain, how do I walk? Dress? Smile? Enter a room?" Though all stock melodramatic villains have common mannerisms, each mime twirls the moustache or swirls the cape differently. Your character may show universal human traits, yet it grows from *your* observations of humanity and will reflect *your* imagination.

Now turn around, and Villain becomes Innocent Victim. In mime, who or what you want to be is all up to you. Turn yourself inside out!

Erase a Face

Assume a neutral face.
Hold your hand next to your face, close but not touching.

Slowly draw your hand across your face,
changing your expression to fear. Keep your eyes focused straight ahead, oblivious to your moving hand.

Erase fear,
slowly moving your hand back across your face. Return to neutral.

Repeat the hand movement,
revealing a different expression each time your hand passes over. Make the changes complete and precise (no smirking or giggling in neutral). How quickly can you create and erase your face?

Try this with a partner,
slowly passing your hand over their neutral face to change it.

Masquerade

Visualize five masks,
all lying on a table in front of you:
Surprise, Anger, Arrogance, Tragedy,
Comedy. Pick up Surprise and look it
over.

Put on Surprise,
while your hands are in front of your
face. Remove your hands, revealing
the mask in place. Tense your face to
maintain the expression as you turn
your head left and right.

Remove Surprise—
changing your face back to neutral
behind your hands—and return it to
the table. Select Anger and put it on.
Return it and try Arrogance.

**Try on Tragedy and Comedy
alternately.**
See how quickly you can switch the
two.

Have one mask get stuck on your face.
Try pulling it off. Insert your finger tips behind the edge of the mask to pry it off. Keeping your head and hands in place, move your shoulders and arms forward, your chest back as you pry.

It's off!
Back to normal you (which one?)

Habits

Put-ons

First dress as yourself.
Reach for your underwear. Step in; pull up. Snap the elastic of your jockey shorts. Pop your head through your undershirt. Fiddle with your bra clasp.

Put on your blouse or shirt.
Slide your arm through the sleeve by holding your body in place and stretching your arm way out. Rotate your shoulder as the fabric comes over it. A quick twist of the fingers puts a button through the hole.

Step into your pants.
Point your toe as your foot goes through the pant leg, sticking out your heel when you get to the bottom. Wriggle the fabric up and over your rear end. Pull up at the waist—hop—and button. Zip up.

Pull on your socks,
toes wiggling as the fabric covers your foot. Lace, tie, or buckle your shoes, boots, or sandals. (Hint: you don't have to lace all twenty eyes on your commando boots—do a few and suggest the rest.)

Now dress as a particular character.

Magicians wear top hats (with rabbits in them); little old ladies wear delicate spectacles; old men wear suspenders that snap; musketeers wear fluffy ostrich feathers in grandiose hats; motorcycle dudes wear leathers with lots of zippers. Just pull the appropriate clothing out of the air!

Reveal your character as you dress.

Feel what an old lady feels when she dons her specs, or a biker as he zips into his leathers, and let your movements suit your feelings. As you dress you are creating your character. New details will emerge as you 'become' your character.

Now undress and try a new character!

A Day in the Life

Mime through a day in the life of a specific character.
Leap out of bed—or drag your body out on the wrong side. Eat your breakfast daintily or with the gusto of a champion. Check the newspaper for today's headlines. Type at the office or dig a trench. As the day closes, go out on the town, settle in with a good book, or crash in an exhausted heap. It all depends upon whom you have chosen to be.

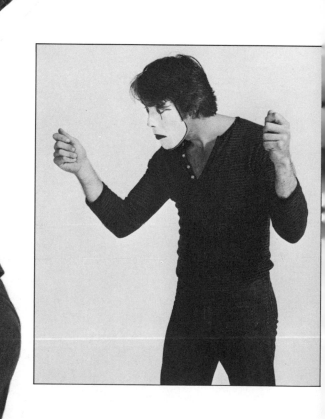

On the Bus

Stand on a street corner, waiting for the bus.
Be any character but yourself—a businessman, senior citizen, mother, toddler, teeny bopper.

Get on the bus when the driver pulls up.
Pay and take a seat.

Explore the bus.
Walk down the center aisle, hang from the overhead strap, look out the window. Remember to stay in character. (Be careful not to put your elbow through the side of the bus when you take your seat!)

Follow your driver's lead.
Vibrate your body with the motor; stop when it's turned off. Lean with the driver as he goes around curves and over bumps. Jerk with the stops and starts.

Signal to get off.
Exit, still in character.

Props

Pass the Prop

Sit in a circle with several other people.
Everyone face the center.

Using a smooth stick as a prop, create a character doing something.
Let the prop suggest or enhance your illusion rather than dominate it—Captain Hook peering through his spyglass, Griselda riding her magic broom, the Pied Piper playing his flute.

Pass the prop on.
Whoever accepts it, use it first as she received it, then change it into something new.

Try other props.
A hoop can become a steering wheel or a puddle. A dish towel can become a bullfighter's cape or a magic carpet.

Boob Tube

Sit in a real chair.
Using an invisible prop—a TV—you are going to watch a series of programs. Your reactions to each one will reveal something about your character; your body movements will indicate what program is on the tube.

Reach over and turn on the TV.
Focus with interest on the program, the zillionth rerun of Cops and Robbers. Get into a shoot-out with the screen as the action mounts. Too violent! Switch the channel.

Turn the dials to adjust the picture.
Lean forward in your chair as you enjoy a tennis match. With your eyes and a slight nod of your head follow the ball back and forth across the net. Root for your favorite—silently.

Catch your wind and switch channels again.

A soap opera. Misty eyed, you settle in for a bit of romance. Your body goes limp, your face sympathetic, maudlin; this is entertainment? Aha, some action!

Get bored with a commercial.
Mock the announcer. Slouch in your chair as you doze off.

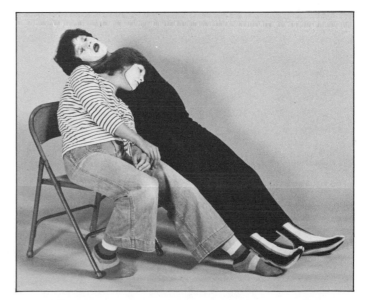

Restaurant

Let one prop help you create all the characters in a restaurant:

The Customer

The Waiter

The Chef

The Dishwasher

Split Personalities

Two People

Begin as a 'short' person.
Turn to your left and look up into the face of an illusory 'tall' person.

Slowly turn back to your right.
When you turn, you grow tall. As the tall person, lower your gaze to look down into the face of the short person you just were. As you alternate characters, be sure you look up or down to the same point in space each time.

Now revolve completely around as you switch characters.
While your back is to the audience, change your facial expression. Experiment with basic opposites—happy and sad, menacing and frightened, lecturing and penitent, angry and apologetic, lovelorn and uninterested.

Give and Take

Create two characters.
One will be the giver and the other the receiver.

Begin as the giver.
Create an object. Turn to your right and hand the object to your illusory receiver.

Revolve to your right.
While your back is to the audience, change your hand positions and facial expressions to become the receiver. Be sure to receive the same object that was offered and from the same place in space.

Throw a punch at your second character.
Revolve to receive the blow.

Kiss your alter ego.
Revolve to receive it. (Narcissism!)

Rescue

Create two characters.
One of them, weak and helpless, is trapped below ground. The other, strong and adventuresome, will come to the rescue.

The strong character is walking above ground.
He hears a cry for help. Where is it coming from? He listens intently.

The weak character is crouched in a hole,
calling out in the hope that someone will hear.

'Strong' puts his ear to the ground,
then starts digging furiously. (He can use an illusory shovel, or even his hands.)

'Weak' extends his hand; 'Strong' keeps digging.
Each time you change characters, revolve once to clearly indicate the switch.

The moment of rescue:
'Strong' reaches down and, keeping his hand in the same spot, revolves to become the weak character being pulled up to safety. (The success of the illusion depends on your maintaining a sense of the vertical separation between the two characters.)

Roseland

With trepidation, clutching her purse, the Timid Soul ascends the stairs to the Roseland Ballroom. She approaches the door, hesitates, knocks. *Whoosh!* The door flies open to reveal the dashing, debonair, determined gigolo. He reaches for her coat. She prefers to remove it herself. Sheepishly, she pays the fee, and the dance begins. A stiff two-step. (Not so close, please!). A wobbly waltz. (Whoops, we're touching!). A torrid tango, with dip no less. (What am I doing in this position?) A kiss. (I like it! I like it!) The no longer Timid Soul moves out! A samba . . . a jitterbug . . . a hustle . . . a . . . tap on the shoulder. Time's up. The Timid Soul deflates. Her former self, she puts on her coat, slumps out the door and down the stairs. Turning her back, she plods away. (But I'll be back next week!)

FIVE

Nuances

Now you've got the picture: mime is trickery by consensus!
Everybody knows that's not your arm sneaking out from
behind your back—it's a snake. Nobody sees the ball
you've tossed into the basket, but everyone knows it's good for
two points. You've agreed to play together.

Nuances are a way to add color to your illusions. Instead of
just drawing a razor across your face to suggest shaving, watch
what's really happening and emphasize that action. Nuances
aren't gimmicks as much as new ways of seeing simple activities
and objects. Some arise from close observation of your body's
dynamics. What happens when someone grabs you by the collar
and yanks you off the scene? You don't expect to go that way, so
half of you remains in place. It's how your *body* expresses the
surprise, as well as your face, that inspires the appropriate mime
gesture.

Sometimes exaggerating a characteristic aspect of an action
shows clearly what you're doing. When you're singing, the vibrato
is happening inside your throat. If you mime that action, you can
call attention to the warble by wiggling your head or your Adam's
apple. Other illusions come from isolating a unique action. Looked
at simply, a butterfly is a fluttering. You don't need wings and
antennae. Your fingers fluttering as your hand circles through the
air is enough.

While you're working out your routines or just playing
around, ideas and gestures will pop up. Use them. Just as no two

mimes look alike, move alike, or think alike, neither do they have
the same imaginations. What you come up with will be your own
unique style.

Growing

As you grow from seed to flower, isolate one part of your body and sprout from there. Try your elbow; your toe instead of your finger.

Shaving

As your razor scrapes across your stubble, stretch your face *away* from the blade. Your chin goes up as the blade comes down.

Toothbrushing

When you're brushing your teeth, move your tongue along the inside of your cheek to indicate where the brush is in your mouth. Be sure you're leaving space between your lips for the toothbrush. Coordinating the movements of your hand holding the brush and your tongue is the real trick here.

Smoking

Inflate and lift your chest for the inhale, deflate and lower for the exhale. Always leave a little hole between your lips for the cigarette, then the smoke. Blow smoke rings, quickly forming an 'O' with your lips and simultaneously dropping your chin for each circle. Let your eyebrows announce each puff.

Drinking

When you're holding a glass or bottle, keep your fingers in place around it. Tilt your head back as you quaff your beverage. Puff out your cheeks with air as you slosh the liquid around inside your mouth. Swallow, bobbing your head up and down with each gulp. Hiccup! Jerk your torso up, then your head, as the hiccup gets sucked in.

Sitting in a Chair

Maintaining a straight back, bend your knees just to the point where you can comfortably keep your balance. Cross your legs at the ankle, or place an ankle on your opposite knee. (At first, you might feel more like an advanced yogi than a person relaxing in a chair!)

Leaning on a Mantle

Place your elbow on the mantle and lean your torso in the same direction. Your legs and hips remain straight. Let your hand dangle freely from the wrist. Prop your head on your hand. Pretend the mantle is the bar at a saloon and order a drink. Whatever you decide to do with your hand, your illusion depends upon keeping your elbow solidly in place or returning it to the same height.

Singing

When you sing, do more than open your mouth. Lift your chest. Wiggle your head with the vibrato. If you have an adam's apple, throw your head back and wiggle that too. Low notes come out best if you think low—pull your chin down and furrow your brow. For high notes, lift your eyebrows and chin high.

Dancing

Try a stylized waltz, tango, or foxtrot *without* touching. ("Darling, something has come between us.")

Come-on

Begin with your right arm around the waist of your illusory girlfriend. You're hopeful as your fingers inch up her side. Rejected, your fingers and face drop. As you revolve to re-enact the scene as the girl, bring your left hand behind you and place it around your waist on the right. (Now it's your boyfriend's arm.) Slowly 'his' fingers inch up your side. With an outraged look, use your right hand to push his hand down. (If you give him a slap, remember you get it, too!)

Making Out

With your back to the audience, wrap your arms around yourself. As you bend your head forward in a passionate kiss, your 'lover's' arms caress your back, squeeze your shoulders, play with your hair. Come up for air with a glance over your shoulder to your audience.

Snake

Your undulating arm is the snake.
Begin with it behind your back. Have
it slowly wriggle out. Your hand—
the snake's head—vibrates for a hiss.

Butterfly

With one hand you can make a butterfly. Keep your fingers straight as you flutter them, moving your hand up, down, and in circles through the air. As the butterfly comes to rest on your finger, your shoulder, or someone's nose, your fingers stop fluttering and start undulating together in a slow rhythm. As the butterfly flies off, jiggle your head slightly as you follow its fluttering, circular flight.

Finish Line

A switch—the contestants run in place as the finish line moves toward them! The two people holding the line move closer and closer to the racers until one runner surges forward to leap the line or break the tape with a swelling chest. The Winner!

Tightrope Wobbling

As you inch your way across an illusory tightrope, flex your knees to indicate the spring of the rope. (Then no one will mistake you as taking a sobriety test.)

Lion Taming

Use a folding chair as a prop to ward
off a fierce feline. Once you've
tamed him, just turn the chair
around—and put your head in the
lion's mouth!

Balloon Flight

Stand with your knees slightly bent.
The balloon you're holding on a
string starts pulling your arm up,
stretching it higher and higher. Your
body follows up . . . up . . . up . . . to
your tip toes. You're floating in
space. Look down to see how far
you've come (about three inches!).

Swordfighting

Having trouble getting your sword out of its scabbard? Keep your hands steady as you pull through your shoulders. *En garde! Touché!* Show the point of contact, and a bit of resistance as you plunge your sword through your victim.

Leaping

When you're jumping off a wall or leaping from a cliff, do it in place. Show you've come a long way by landing crouched on deeply flexed knees. Rise slowly to standing. If you're doing a smaller jump, bend your knees less. Always land on the balls of your feet to avoid a loud and distracting thud.

Flying

Poised on the ball of your foot, rotate your body freely in all directions. Move your head, shoulders, hips, knees. Dip, sway, change feet, use both feet. Glide with your arms out to the side. (Flap them, and you'll look like a bird.) Look down to show how high you are.

Stuck Door

If you pull your hand back and forth trying to open a stuck door, you've created an elastic doorknob! Instead, keep your hand stationary, and jerk back and forth through your chest to create the 'pull'.

Getting Stuck

Bump into someone or something as
if it were sticky. At the point of
contact, *push* while the rest of your
body appears to pull away,
struggling to get unstuck.

Surprise Exit

Remember the slapstick routine,
"Hey, get that guy off the stage!"?
Try it. Stand with your head turned
to one side. From the opposite
direction, a hand appears (yours) and
hooks a finger into your imaginary
shirt collar. Yank! As you turn your
surprised face to the audience, your
head and hips jerk in the opposite
direction of the pull. Off you go!

The Prisoner

Inside a very small box, the Mime crouches. Cautiously, she explores her prison, hands touching sides, top, bottom. She pushes with her back, with her feet, with her hands. Pushes harder, pushes stronger. Tension. And release! The sides of the box fall away around her, and she's free. Free! Slowly she stands and steps from her broken prison. A few tentative steps, a skip, then a stride. Jubilant, her movements expand and grow carefree. She spins and runs forward. *Bam!* Her hands flatten against the unexpected wall. Her body jerks taut at the impact. Bewildered. Slowly, hand after hand, she follows the wall, meets a corner and turns. Follows another wall to another corner. Moving frantically now, she follows to another corner and another. A box. She pounds and pushes desperately. Exhausted, she leans against the wall. And slowly it moves in toward her. Apprehensive, she runs to another wall. It too is slowly moving inward. And the others. With her whole body, with all her strength, she tries to hold them back. The Mime is last seen crouched inside a very small box.

SIX

Make-up

The mimes of ancient Rome whitened their faces with flour and outlined their features with charcoal. Erasing individuality, one character could play many parts. Facial expression could be clearly seen, even at a distance, by the audiences that filled the great arena.

Today's mimes use more sophisticated make-up, but the reasons for using it remain the same—to let 'Everyman' be seen by his audience. Rather than defining a happy face or a sad face, the mask of a clown or a villain, classic mime make-up creates a neutral face that can express all emotions, all characters. As 'Everyman', the mime can be 'Anyman'! However, even masking individual features with classic whiteface does not erase the uniqueness of the performer beneath. Accented by whiteface, even the most subtle facial movement—the rise of a brow, a wrinkle of the mouth—can be seen at a distance. (Never wink in whiteface unless you mean it!)

The more often you make up, the better you'll get to know your own bumps and creases, curves and hollows, and the easier it will become. Allow yourself at least a half hour for your first session. You might find it easier to have someone else help, especially with drawing the lines. Besides, exploring someone else's face is as much a discovery as exploring your own.

You don't have to wear whiteface to do mime. You've been doing fine without it! But you might want to experiment. Making up is an experience in itself. In whiteface, your jawbone and cheekbones suddenly appear, your eyes expand, your nose takes shape. Everything washes off, except the look of satisfaction at seeing yourself in a new way.

Make-up Kit

What you'll need.

The materials you need to create your classic whiteface are few and simple. Clown white or mime white comes as either a cream or a pancake to be applied with a damp sponge. Substitutes such as tempera paint just don't work. They crack and flake, and they're bad for your skin. For your mouth you need theatrical foot rouge in light red or a bright red commercial lipstick. If you are going to be working under stage lights, use a darker cherry red. For outlining your eyebrows, lips, and face, use a simple eyebrow pencil or black liquid eyeliner and brush. If you don't have theatrical powder, baby powder works to set your mask. When you're ready to take it off, soap and water will do the job; paper towels and make-up remover may speed things up.

Where to get it.

Your local theater supply store or any eclectic drugstore should carry everything you will need. If not, you can order mime make-up by mail (*see* Resources, page 190).

Preparation

Dress in an old shirt.
This protects your costume from smudges. Pin your hair back with bobby pins, removing them when you've finished making up.

Look at your face in the mirror.
Relax. With your fingertips, trace your jawbone from ear to ear. Continue up along your hairline and back to your ear. If you are bald, experiment with a natural outline where your hairline would be. You have outlined your 'mask of silence'.

Splash your face with cold water to close the pores.
Dry your face.

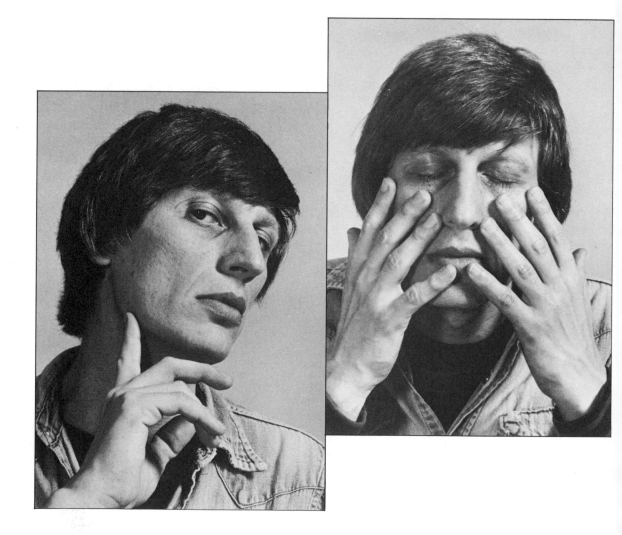

Whiteface

Take a small amount of clown white on your fingertips.
Spread it on your face, starting at your hairline and moving down. Smooth it on evenly, but no thicker than is needed to cover your skin color. With practice, you'll discover how much you need to use. Cover your eyebrows and eyelids but not your lashes. Bring the make-up as close to your lower lashes as is comfortable. If you have a moustache, go around it, leaving it natural.

Smooth out the stroke lines.
Wipe off any excess white with a damp towel or make-up remover. Clean up any stray white on your neck, ears, or hairline before continuing. Neatness is important in creating the simplicity of traditional white face.

Dab on white powder to set the cream.
This is particularly necessary if you will be performing under heavy lights. Remove the excess powder with a cotton ball or soft make-up brush.

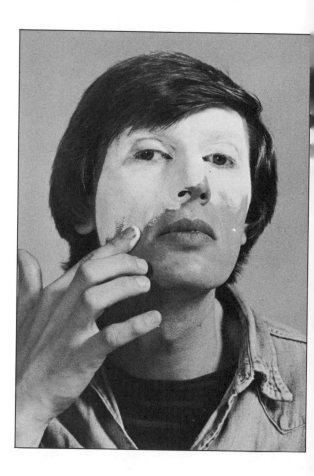

Eyes

Create your new eyebrows.

Using your fingernail, scratch in arches above your own eyebrows. Crooked? Smooth over and try again. When the two arches match, fill in the line with a stroke of black eyebrow pencil or black liquid eyeliner. As you grow adept, you will be able to dispense with the fingernail guidelines.

Outline your eyes.

Draw a line across the upper lid following your lashes. Extend the line slightly out to the side. Repeat on the lower lid at the lash line, extending the line out and upward at the corner and connecting with the line on the upper lid.

Draw a vertical line above and below your eyes.

Start the line just below your real eyebrow (now covered with whiteface) and continue it to approximately an equal distance below your eye. Since the muscles around your eyes contract when you close your eyes, you should draw these lines with your eyes open; then connect the upper and lower lines with a line across your closed eyelid.

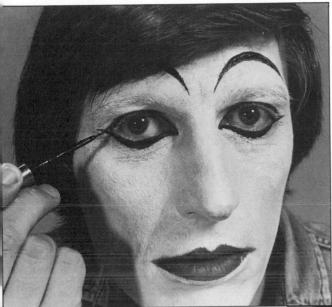

Mouth

Outline your mouth.
Here's a chance to change nature!
Look at your total face. Create a
mouth in proportion to your other
new features. If you have a small
mouth, make it slightly larger. If
you have a large mouth, reduce it
by outlining in black only as much
as you wish to show and covering
the rest in white. Either way, be
sure to keep the corners of your
mouth *narrow* and slightly turned
up.

**Fill in the outline of your
mouth with red.**
Blot.

Mask

Outline your whiteface with a black line.
This line should follow and enhance the natural shape of your face. Your 'mask of silence' is now complete.

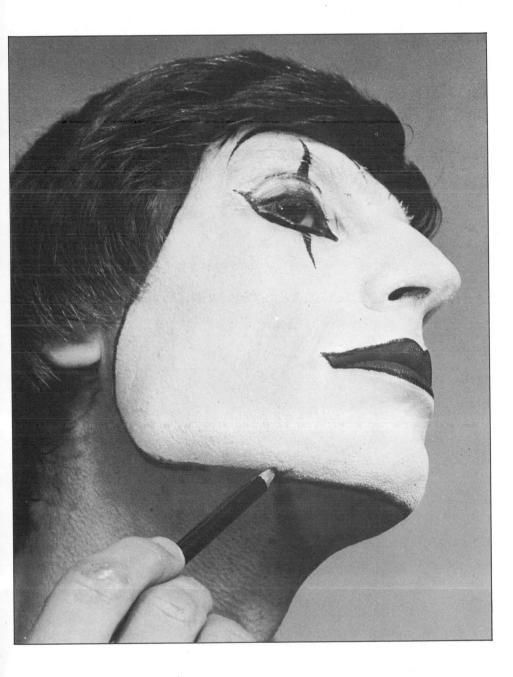

Exploration

Spend some time in front of a mirror.

You may be surprised by the transformation. (Is that me?) You'll not only look different, you'll feel different, inside and out. Some people become more relaxed as soon as their own face has disappeared. That one-millimeter layer of white cream seems to create a psychological incognito.

Experiment.

How many different kinds of smiles can you now make? What does your face say when you raise your brows? When you drop the corners of your mouth? Wearing whiteface is like donning a moveable mask. Every facial movement takes on a new quality—clear and amplified. You may be surprised to find out how many moveable masks you really have.

Cleaning up.

Wipe off as much of your make-up as possible with a tissue or a ball of cotton. Then wash your face with soap and water. You'll probably have to do this two or three times to get everything off.

Performing

If tossing invisible balls to a friend, riding off into the sunset alone, or developing smiles for your mirror leaves you asking for more, you may want to perform! Maybe a friend has asked you to come to his child's birthday party as a mime. Maybe you've decided to dramatize an ecological issue at your club's benefit. Maybe you and your friends want to try out some mime in the park. You're ready to take up the challenge of communicating with or entertaining an audience. Performing isn't necessarily the culmination of your mime experience; just doing mime for yourself and enjoying it might be all you want. But if you do decide to perform, here are a few pointers to make sharing your fantasy more effective—and fun.

Your half hour or so on stage can require hours of preparation. Besides creating and rehearsing your routines, you'll also be dealing with costumes, perhaps make-up and equipment, and with other people. Your routine can be based on anything from fairy tales to politics, from your personal experiences to the fate of humanity. You may want to perform in classic whiteface make-up—the mime mystique. Creating your mime face and choosing a comfortable costume is an important part of your preparation. How you perform your routine will also depend on where you are presenting it—on a stage, in someone's living room, in a park, on the street.

Wherever you choose, the surest way to make your performance work is to be prepared. Know what you want to say and how you want to say it. With good preparation you can turn that state of heightened energy known as stage fright to your advantage. That little quiver in your knees or inside your stomach can give you the extra energy you need to give out to a lot of people all at once. Knowing your routine thoroughly is like walking a familiar street—your body knows where to go, leaving your mind free to explore and adjust to your changing surroundings.

The more tangible your mime experience is for you—whether that means really feeling that invisible ball in your hand or experiencing the terror of being trapped inside a box—the more real it will be for your audience. You're offering a part of yourself, revealing something about who you are and how you see your world. Performing makes you vulnerable, but it can be a risk well worth taking. Spontaneous laughter, thoughtful silences, applause— you've communicated.

Routines

A good routine has a focus. It presents one clear situation or makes one specific point. When you begin to create your routine, decide first what it is that you want to communicate, what theme you want to explore. Ask yourself what experience you intend to offer your audience. You may want them to giggle or to be pensive, to relax or cheer.

In deciding how to get your idea across, consider who is to receive it. A four-year-old may not understand a routine designed for a forty-year-old, and vice versa. You don't have to compromise your message; rather, select details common to the experience of your audience. If you are in doubt about what might be appropriate, offer a challenge rather than 'talk down' to your audience. It's exhilarating to unearth latent sensitivity.

CHOOSING A SUBJECT

There may be many things you want to 'discuss' through a routine,

but they have to surface. Draw upon your own experience. Your daily life has countless incidents of fate and humor that others can relate to. You could illustrate a losing battle with machines (The Typewriter Shuffle or The Freeway Blues). Consider the delights and doldrums of your job as a theme. You might do a routine on The Midnight Snack and stealthily indulge in a sumptuous feast. Explore characters you are familiar with—The Babysitter, The Professor, The Guru, The Burglar, The Ballet Teacher, The Garbage Collector.

Fairy tales and myths can be a rich source of inspiration. Since your audience already knows the story, you are free to give your own interpretation. Maybe you'd like to change the ending and have the Wolf eat Little Red Riding Hood after all! Or create the Universal Pig (mightier than three little ones) and have him blow down the Wolf. You can be both Dr. Jekyll and Mr.

Hyde, Robin Hood and Maid Marian. You can be Alice at a tea party of invisible guests, or with a group of friends you can silently bring alive the snoring Dormouse and the mercurial Mad Hatter. With myths and fairy tales, you're free to improvise and interpret your *own* fantasy.

The same goes for working with themes based on standard melodrama. The Old West, The Sawmill, Over the Falls, On the Rails—they're all themes familiar to your audience, so you can put your villain through any paces you choose. (With a bionic heroine, your villain won't stand a chance.)

Try rewriting history. Become a famous figure as he or she really was—in your fantasy. Or take a famous scene and show what could have happened. (Washington sinks crossing the Delaware!)

Your own cosmic commentary can make a good theme for a routine. Try the 'Biggies'— evolution, birth and death, love and rejection, crime and punishment, pollution and ecology, Armageddon or epiphany. You may have seen some of these done by professional mimes. Give them your unique interpretation.

If you are doing a routine with a group of people, exploring environments can be a good starting point. Together decide on a setting; one person can then begin with an appropriate action, and everyone else join in as they are inspired to be someone or something in the setting. At the seashore, you can make sandcastles, play ball, swim, run in the waves—or *be* the waves. On the farm, you can milk cows, feed

Dolphin (Joe McCord) in 'Song for a Dying Whale' at Greenpeace benefit

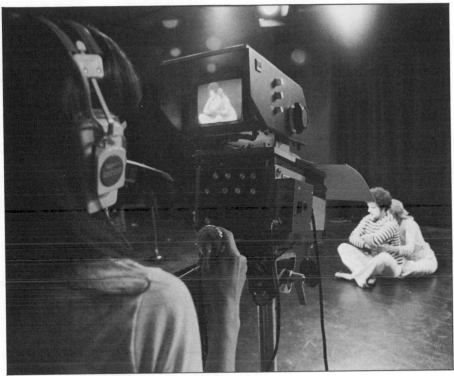

College of Marin Mime/Video Workshop

chickens, toss hay, or be tossed. At the factory, everyone can join in to make a giant machine with cogs, wheels, levers, and pistons. Your machine can start out slowly, get oiled, go wild, grind down, and die. (You might add some jazz or rock music to set the tempo.)

In creating your routine, draw upon the objects and movements you learned in the earlier chapters of this book. If you put together horseback riding and fighting, you can enact a rousing scene from the Old West. As a musketeer, you might use swordfighting, climbing, looking over a wall. Whatever theme you decide to explore, be sure your characters and situation are simple and clear. Your routine should do more than report an experience; it should actually *be* an experience for both the mime and the audience.

STRUCTURING YOUR ROUTINE

Once you've decided on the theme or subject of your routine, begin working with it physically. The routine will develop as you actually do parts of it. Some of the details will come to you in a rush of intuitive feeling, others will arise through thought and analysis. You'll come up with a lot of possibilities from which you can select the details that work.

Your routine will need a beginning, a climax, and an ending. No matter what you're trying to say, it has to include getting you on and off the performing area or clearly indicate the start and completion of your act. However,

you don't need curtains and stage wings in order to 'disappear'. You can begin by facing your audience in neutral or with your head down and conclude by returning to neutral or lowering your head again. Or you can begin and end with your back to the audience.

The climax of your routine is like the punch line. Once you get to it, your statement is made. Everything that follows is a consequence of or a comment on your main point. Make sure the climax is clear. Remember, your audience doesn't know what is going to happen. You have to build up suspense with your feelings as well as your actions and take the audience along with you. Don't make them wait too long. Sneak up to a wall, explore it with your hands. What is waiting on the other side? Look over the top or around the wall. Your reaction will show what you discover.

When you have all the elements of your routine together, start to edit. Try to say the most with the least. Get your point across with your movements and facial expressions. Be sure each one is clear, saying only what you want it to say. If you wave your hand at someone, you're indicating that you're greeting them. But if you wave again, it implies that the person didn't see you, and the gesture takes on a new meaning. Try not to repeat yourself, particularly to milk a response.

You may want to add extra effects to your routine, like sound, lights, or simple props. They're never required—you're enough. But you can experiment to add to the mood, atmosphere, or setting. A drum beat might emphasize your

Giant's footsteps, or rinky-tink music could set the scene for an Old West Saloon. Colored lights can suggest a setting or mood—reds for a hot desert or anguish, blues for a vast expanse or loneliness. However, these additions can also be corny and distracting, so use them with discretion. Special effects are special only if they enhance your illusion without cluttering it.

As a final step in creating your routine, try it out on a friend to get some feedback. Good criticism might be painful and may cause you to make some changes or sacrifice some fond detail, but it can improve your presentation. Rather than asking, "Is this good or bad?" ask "Is this clear? Am I communicating?" The important point is not whether your friend likes the routine, but whether *you* like it and are getting across what you want.

WORKING WITH GROUPS

If you choose to do a routine with a group of people rather than by yourself, cooperation is important. You have to communicate with each other before you can communicate with an audience. It takes extra time, thought, and energy. Spend some time playing and improvising together so you can learn each other's ways and ideas. Enjoy the process.

Input from everyone in the group can be creative and inspiring, but after a certain point it diffuses the energy. Decide which one of you is going to be in charge—this time—and trust that person's judgment.

Clothing

Traditional mime clothing has ranged from flowing silks to mere loincloths. The white robes of the classical Pierrot had full sleeves and pants that enhanced each movement with a graceful swirl. Contemporary mimes use a variety of casual costumes—striped shirts, bell bottoms, tights, suspenders, hats—to create their individual images.

You probably already have suitable clothing in your own closet. A T-shirt with jeans, drawstring cottons, or sailor pants from the Army-Navy surplus can serve the purpose. Avoid patterned materials, such as flowered shirts or plaid pants. The eyes of your audience can be drawn more to your undulating Hawaiian shirt than to your face.

If you want to outline your body as an abstract form, a solid colored outfit such as a jumpsuit or leotard and tights works best.

Robert Shields

Mummenshanz

When you're working against a dark curtain or backdrop, wear something light in color. Keep your costume simple. Adding accessories such as hats, ribbons, or flowers may hamper your versatility. Add peculiar parts to your characters' costumes as you need them—through illusion.

For group work, wearing the same or similar clothing has the effect of focusing the audience's attention on the total action rather than on individual personalities.

How you dress your hands and feet depends on how you want to use them. White cotton gloves can emphasize the movements of your hands, but they might also add a certain flair to your character that you do not intend. Your shoes should be lightweight and flexible. Make sure they can slide easily and silently. Ballet slippers, China cotton slippers, and canvas gym shoes are all useful. If you want to draw attention to your feet, wear white. Otherwise, dark shoes are more practical.

What you adopt as your mime costume will reflect your own style. The main consideration is that your clothing be simple and comfortable, permitting your body to move freely. You want both yourself and your audience to be able to concentrate on what you're doing, not on what you're wearing. Underneath it all, it's the language of your body that counts. Not even the most exquisite of costumes can make the mime.

Presentation

With your preparations complete, you're ready to go at last. Whether performing indoors or outdoors, on a stage or in the street, give yourself fully to your creation. Make the most out of the energy you have put into it.

Work close to your audience. It's easy to unconsciously move upstage, away from them. Know on what part of your body you want the audience to focus and be sure it can be easily seen. Your face is especially important. Often an audience looks to a performer's face to tell the whole story, only peripherally taking in body movements. Present your full face or have at least three-quarters of it turned toward the audience when the focus is on you.

Even when you are facing a partner and your bodies are in profile, your faces should be three-quarters visible. You don't have to look directly at each other—out of the corners of your eyes is enough. Avoid standing slightly behind your partner so he has to turn away from the audience to look at you. Upstaging, as it is called, takes the focus off him and leaves you fully in the 'spotlight'. By moving up next to your partner, you *share* the attention.

If you are not part of the key action at some point but are still on stage, you can best contribute to the scene by not creating a distraction. Direct the attention of the audience toward the main event by focusing your own energy on it. Depending on what's appropriate to the routine, you can fix your gaze on the action, assume a neutral pose, or even turn your back to the audience. When you're working with a group, stay aware of each person and what he or she is doing. Be prepared to improvise

Suggs (Carol Sue Thomas) at the Cannery, San Francisco

supportively if something doesn't go according to plan, but let your action be a tide-over, not a take-over!

Whether you are working by yourself, with a partner, or with a group, use your space fully. Even if you have to remain in one place, you can kneel, squat, bend, lean, sway. Your audience will find it much more interesting if they don't view you at just one height.

PERFORMING ON A STAGE

Your 'stage' may be your friend's living room rug, the gymnasium floor, or the real thing. Wherever your performance is going to take place, try to get in at least one rehearsal there. It's reassuring to be familiar with your surroundings before you perform. You'll also have the chance to deal with any environmental handicaps. (Maybe the handball court is situated in the adjacent room, and you will be accompanied by unsolicited sound effects!) If you can't rehearse on location, visualize yourself in the space and run through your act.

If you plan to use special lighting or sound effects, be sure to rehearse with them. Persuade a friend who knows your routine (preferably inside out) to become your sound and lighting technician. (They might also be willing to tote extension cords, tape recorders, speakers, spotlights, signs, and whatever else you've incorporated into your act.)

To say that something *might* go awry with your equipment could be an understatement. Don't fume if it happens in the middle of your performance. Fake it. Adjust calmly to the situation. Your audience may never notice—especially if they, like you, are concentrating on your work.

PERFORMING ON THE STREET

Presenting your mime routine in the unstructured environment of a park or a street corner has its own particular challenges and rewards. There is no stage barrier between you and your audience. They are an actual part of your act. If you've always wanted to 'talk' with strangers, taking to the streets as a mime may be for you.

Perhaps you have watched a mime on the street responding to audience suggestions, incorporating outsiders into the act. It all looks so spontaneous, improvised. That may very well be part of the illusion. The mime has probably done a

similar routine many times, for her friends or for other audiences. Because she's confident enough about her basic routine, she's free to adjust it to her present gathering, to respond to their reactions, to let something a bit new emerge each time.

Your biggest challenge in doing street mime is to remain flexible. Be prepared to deal with the unexpected. Perhaps you lasso someone, put them on your illusory horse, and plan to ride off into the sunset to end the act, but your new partner starts roping cattle instead. Adjust. Rope a few yourself, while you're thinking of another way to end the act for both of you.

The more people you include in your act at any one time, the trickier it can become. Don't draw more people in than you can handle. It helps to offer each participant something specific to do *before* getting onstage. For your own sake as well as the audience's, be sensitive to who wants to play and who doesn't. Allow people to join in by their own choice—although some like a little encouragement. If what you are doing is inviting, you'll find plenty of people who will want to play, as well as watch.

Children are often your most imaginative and eager participants, ready to accept a freshly-picked invisible flower or join in a ropeless tug-of-war. But approach them gently. Whiteface can be spooky to someone who has never seen it before. A caterwauling child

running from an apologetic mime is an uncomfortable experience for everyone. Then, once you have their trust, watch out! Children have been known to try anything to get a mime to talk—even pinching. Involve their energy in a routine rather than in your torture!

Before you set yourself up on a street corner or in a town park, make sure your environment is safe and comfortable for you and your audience. A busy street corner can be difficult and even dangerous for pedestrians, distracted drivers, and *you*. Respect the wishes of the local citizenry. If a merchant thinks you are hurting his business, move on. You're bound to find one who recognizes you as an attraction. You may need a license to perform in certain areas, particularly if people are throwing money at your feet. (Don't hold your breath waiting for the clink of coins.)

Always keep in mind that you're out on the street to communicate and hopefully entertain—not to shock, mock, or cause a rumpus. If you feel the call of the streets, pull your act together and set out. Walk your dog, as a mime. Go grocery shopping, as a mime. Be prepared to play.

USING SIGNS

While your routine should be able to stand on its own, a title sign can be a valuable addition. With just a few words, you can establish the setting, the tone, or the plot. For example, showing the audience a sign reading "The Snake Charmer" prepares them for what's ahead. When you sit down cross-legged and adjust your illusory turban, they're already in the marketplace

Toad the Mime (Antoinette Attell) at California School for the Deaf

Audiences

Although you can work in various ways to attract audiences to you, don't forget that there are many potential spectators already available and waiting. Gatherings such as auctions, fund-raising campaigns, festivals, and parades have ready-made audiences that love a little entertainment. There are other places, such as hospitals, prisons, and retirement homes, with many people who would welcome the chance to experience live performers. You might check to see if your community has an organization that puts performing groups in touch with interested institutions and place yourself on their circuit.

Above all, remember that as a performer you have something to share. You have not only your act, but also a way of enjoying people and helping them to enjoy themselves. If you keep this as your ultimate purpose and guide, your performances will be successful and mutually rewarding.

with you. All you have to do now is produce the snake.

The best titles are simple and evocative. Rather than telling the whole story ("How I Ate the Shaving Cream this Morning"), the title should set the stage ("Morning Ritual"), or make a leading comment ("Super Suds").

Be sure your sign is large enough and legible. Stiff posterboard at least two feet by one foot is best. Although it's fun to use different styles of lettering, plain block letters are most easily seen. Black lettering on white, with a red and black border line, is clear and effective—and also echoes the colors of your whiteface make-up.

If you're working with a group, presenting the sign can become a mini-act in itself, especially if an appropriate character brings it on.

A forlorn suitor trailing "The Great Love Affair" previews the drama to follow. The 'sign mime' can keep the mood going while other performers change costume or catch a quick breath. However, his act shouldn't detract from his business; the art of sign-carrying is to move slowly and keep the sign positioned so the audience can read it. (Speedy subtitles are frustrating!)

Indoors, the sign is usually shown to the audience and then removed. When you're performing on the street, it's helpful to leave the sign propped nearby to offer latecomers a clue to the routine in progress.

Using signs can provide shortcuts and additional fun and entertainment, but don't rely on your sign or your sign carrier to carry your routine. Use the sign as a clue to set off your audience's imagination rather than to explain what you're doing.

Teaching

Whether you're a teacher by profession or your 'class' is your family or friends gathered for the evening, when you become a mime mentor, you are not only imparting information but also drawing out creativity. This happens best in a supportive environment. In your enthusiasm to communicate the delights of mime, take time to put yourself in the place of those you are teaching. Imagine yourself as the new learner and work to make the experience feel good. No one likes to be embarrassed, put on the spot, or feel awkward (nor is it a necessary rite of passage). If you have decided to share mime either informally or by conducting a class, the following suggestions may be worthwhile.

Before you get together with your group, have something specific to share and know where you are going. Prepare more material than you think you'll need (in case you have a very motivated group), but don't feel you have to rush to get through everything you've decided to do. Your structure should provide a solid but flexible platform. Depending on your experience, your preparation time will probably take about as long as your actual class time.

Just because you're teaching silent communication, you needn't feel self-conscious about using words to keep the class going. It's reassuring to students to hear simple directions as a voice-over. Avoid delivering a lot of history and philosophy, and get into *doing*. You may eventually want to try conducting an entire class completely in silence. It can be more difficult, but once everyone catches on, things can move even more fluidly. It's like taking a French class entirely in French—the communication and instruction is direct, and you don't have to translate. Moreover, twenty minutes to an hour or two of active silence is a rare experience.

Always begin with warm-ups. Create the opportunity to put aside verbal habits, to loosen up (inside and outside), and to gather personal energies to focus on something new. Starting a class with "Let's act out our fantasies— you first!" is a sure disaster. The person called upon may not even realize he *has* a fantasy.

Progress slowly, from individual exercises, to group work, to performing. After warming up, begin with the group seated and doing something small—a ball, a box, a butterfly—before asking them to leave the security of their places to try the walls or the walks. Concentrating on a specific exercise allows everyone to relate to their own work first. No one is watching; no one feels put on the spot.

Then break into partners. Doing the Mirror or the Marionette as a warm-up for partners is a painless and enjoyable bridge from working alone to exploring technique together. You'll feel your group relaxing as they get to know each other as individuals. Then you're ready to form small groups and try something like prop passing. People are watching each other now, but it's a game, not a 'performance'. Still in small groups, work on something requiring teamwork, such as the Tug of War, Ship Ahoy, or Pushing Over a Wall.

Only when people are relatively comfortable with doing something before the eyes of the group should you offer an optional performance assignment. Suggest a TV commercial or a short melodrama. While it might be less complicated for an individual to work alone, it is often more comfortable to perform along with a group of people. Keep early group assignments simple, since it's easy to get involved in verbal planning and discussion rather than in doing.

Guide the review and discussion of performances toward supportive commentary. Rather than judging a presentation as good or bad, ask the observers what they liked about it. There are always a few good moments. Then, if necessary, offer suggestions on how to make the communication more clear next time. Be wary of the 'star' syndrome. Every class will have someone who excels. He or she can

easily become a discouragement rather than an inspiration to the others. Look for and acknowledge the progress made by each person.

In demonstrating techniques and ideas to students, be careful not to become the star yourself. If you find your students copying you instead of creating their own illusions, play less yourself and observe more. When they're once again drawing upon their own resources, join in.

Keep the activity level of each class varied. A series of physically active exercises should be followed by a calming down period to give your students a chance to relax, recoup, and reflect. Try to wrap up each session with a feeling of personal accomplishment for each student. Don't introduce something like a difficult walk as the last activity. It's better to end with

everyone doing something familiar or as a group sharing energy.

The first time your students apply whiteface will be an experience in itself. Allow plenty of time and be prepared for a mess! (Remind them to wear an old shirt over their clothes.) It's difficult for a beginner to draw the lines on his own face, and it can be very disappointing to see himself turn out with wiggly eyebrows and a monster mouth. You might help out with the lines and encourage students to draw them for each other once they get the idea. Although beginners are likely to overdo the make-up on the first try, it will be a great opportunity for them to explore their own and each other's faces.

When you introduce make-up for the first time, have more available for students to take with them for further exploration on their own. Suggest that they wear their new faces home and communicate silently for as long as they can.

If you have access to one, a videotape recorder can be a great mime teaching aid. Students benefit from the instant feedback they get as to what they're really communicating when they're a part of their own audience. It's also a good way for students to watch their own progress. (Besides, it's fun to see yourself on TV!) You might want to use the tapes of finished routines as entertainment for another class, the noisy lunch room, parents' night, or a rainy day.

Ultimately, it's not how much material you cover in a class as much as what you have created in the process. Let the experience be a playful one. Learn from each other, enjoy each other, share your illusions and your fantasies!

Kay Hamblin and students

Lesson Plan

The following plan indicates how you might organize a six-week class for your students. Use it as a suggestion or guideline, keeping in mind that each class will have its own particular requirements.

Each week begins with the Big X as a familiar way to get into silence, followed by other warm-ups, review, and new material. Each session ends with a game for the entire group.

The lesson plan has been designed to introduce progressively more difficult techniques each week. Some, such as walking, are reviewed by re-teaching them the following week. Other techniques, such as Boxes, are reviewed less formally through games such as Gifts or Movers.

The activities suggested for each lesson are in a sequence that offers variety and change of pace. There are exercises and games for individuals, partners, and small groups. Some material involves broad and active movement, and some requires activity to be done sitting down or in a quiet mood. Each lesson could last from an hour to an afternoon, depending upon the energy and concentration of your group.

In this lesson plan, make-up is not introduced until the fifth session. Usually by that time, students have realized that it is themselves and not a mask that is creating the illusion.

If you assign creative 'homework', request your students to prepare the routines for the following class, but let it be optional whether they actually present them or not. Performing can be done in small groups or before the entire class, depending upon what feels best.

In the following lists, exercises marked (P) are for partners; those marked (G) are for groups. An asterisk (*) indicates a review from a previous lesson. Numbers following listings are page references to this book.

ONE

Big X 25
Neutral 26
Hands Up 28
Magic Shoes 32
Midnight Snack 38
Mirror (P) 40
Face Passing (G) 41
Creating a Ball 49
Exploring a Ball 50
Tossing a Ball (P) 51
Easy Walk 81
Follow the Leader (G) 86
Erase a Face 113
Put-ons 116
Shaving 136
Toothbrushing 137
Smoking 138
Drinking 139
Leaning on a Mantle 141
Request routines based on daily life for next week.
Ball Games 52

TWO

Big X* 25
Neutral* 26
Hands Up* 28
Magic Shoes* 32
Robot 34
Mirror* (P) 40
Face Passing* (G) 41
Ball Games* (G) 52
Creating a Table Top 54
Hitting a Table 55
Moving Tables (P) 56
Easy Walk* 81
Sliding Walk 82
Follow the Leader* (G) 86
Rope Pull 101
Erase a Face* 113
A Day in the Life 118
Sitting in a Chair 140
Singing 142
Dancing 143
Stuck Door 156
Perform routines based on daily life.
Request routines based on melodrama for next week.
Tug of War (G) 102

THREE

Big X* 25
Neutral* 26
Marionette (P) 30
Mirror* (P) 40
Creating a Box 64
Lifting a Box 66
Opening a Box 67
Easy Walk* 81
Sliding Walk* 82
Profile Walk 84
Follow the Leader* (G) 86
Subway 87
Masquerade 114
Boob Tube (P) 122
Restaurant 124
Two People 126
Snake 146
Butterfly 147
Getting Stuck (G) 157
Perform routines based on melodrama.
Request routines based on re-written history for next week.
Movers (G) 68

Resources

Books

The Mime Book
Claude Kipnis
Harper and Row / New York / 1974
$12.50 hardbound; $6.95
paperbound
A detailed presentation of technique
for the serious and committed
student. Illustrated with photographs.

Mime, The Technique of Silence
Richmond Shepard
Drama Book Specialists / New York /
1971
$7.50 hardbound (text edition)
Technique and exercises explained in
thirty lessons. Illustrated with line
drawings.

Improvisation for the Theatre
Viola Spolin
Northwestern University Press /
Evanston, Illinois / 1963
$7.50 hardbound (text edition)
The classic collection of theater
games for actors and people who
just want to play.

Behind the Mask
Bari Rolfe
Persona Books / Oakland, California /
1977
$2.95 paperbound
An introduction to using the mask,
with suggested exercises. Illustrated
with photographs.

Clowns
John Towsen
Hawthorn Books / New York / 1976
$14.95 hardbound
A survey of clowns throughout
history that explores the
development and relationship
between clown and mime. Illustrated
with a wide variety of historical and
contemporary drawings and
photographs.

The San Francisco Mime Troupe: The First Ten Years
R. G. Davis
Ramparts Press / Palo Alto,
California / 1975
$14.00 hardbound; $3.95
paperbound
From "Beginnings" to "Guerilla
Resident Radical," the growth of one
political theater company as well as a
perspective on the political theater
movement.

Marcel Marceau, Master of Mime
Ben Martin
Paddington Press / Grosset and
Dunlap / New York / 1978
$12.95 hardbound
A visual biography of the world's
best known mime. Color and black
and white photographs of Marceau
on stage, off stage, in the studio,
and at home.

Periodicals/Directories

The following publications are available from International Mimes and Pantomimists, Route Three, Spring Green, Wisconsin 53588.

I.M.P. Newsletter
$6.00 per year; $9.00 for libraries and institutions
A bi-monthly newsletter announcing and reviewing mime events.

Mime Journal
$7.00 per year; $14.00 for libraries and institutions
A magazine published twice yearly. Each issue is devoted to one aspect of mime or closely related theater. Illustrated with photographs.

Mime Directory
Volume 1: Human Resources
1977
$5.00; $7.50 for libraries and institutions
A directory of mimes around the world, cross-referenced alphabetically and by region. Performance and course descriptions and addresses make this a useful tool.

Mime Directory
Volume 2: Bibliography
1978
$5.00; $7.50 for libraries and institutions
A detailed listing of books, articles, and films relevant to mime and pantomime.

Films

The following films can be rented by individuals, groups, schools, and media centers. Check your local library or university film rental before you write for information.

The Art of Silence: Pantomimes with Marcel Marceau
Encyclopedia Brittanica Films
425 North Michigan Avenue
Chicago, Illinois
8–17 minutes; color
In a series of thirteen short films, Marceau introduces mime and performs some of his most famous pantomimes (The Maskmaker, Bip Hunts Butterflies, Bip at a Society Party). The next best to seeing a live performance by this famous artist.

In the Park
AIMS Instructional Media Services
626 Justin Avenue
Glendale, California 91201
14 minutes; black and white
Using a few simple props and much imagination, Marceau populates a park with characters. Inventive, fun, and instructive for the observant student.

A Night at the Peking Opera
Radim Films
17 West 60th Street
New York, New York 10023
20 minutes; color
Using traditional music and costumes, the Chinese Opera creates a celebration of opera, pantomime, acrobatics, and imagination.

The Comedies of Charlie Chaplin
Films Incorporated
1144 Wilmette Avenue
Wilmette, Illinois 60091
30 minutes each; black and white
Any of Chaplin's films are a mime's delight. The dozen 'two-reelers' of the Mutual Series (1916–1917) are particularly instructive since Chaplin was developing his techniques in such shorts as *The Floorwalker, The Rink, Easy Street.* For a full-length film exposure, see *Modern Times* (89 minutes; black and white), featuring Chaplin at his famous assembly line routine.

Children of Paradise (Les Enfants du Paradis)
Films Incorporated
1144 Wilmette Avenue
Wilmette, Illinois 60091
188 minutes; black and white
Completed in 1945, this feature directed by Marcel Carne is the classic film on mime. It is a fictional biography of the nineteenth century mime Deburau. Jean-Louis Barrault is an unforgettable image as the whitefaced Pierrot. An exploration of love, theater, and illusion.

Make-up

The Mime Kit
Box 568
Ross, California 94957
$6.50 postpaid
The Mime Kit includes 'clown' white, red lip rouge, black professional eyeliner, make-up remover, and directions. One kit should make up about twenty-five faces.

Index

Edited by Andrew Fluegelman .
Designed by Howard Jacobsen

Text edited by Shoshana Tembeck
Additional photography by
    Basil Hamblin
Photographic printing by
    Chong Lee
Make-up by Lester Barnett

Set in Frutiger 45/46/75 by
    Chapman's Phototypesetting,
    Fullerton, California
Production by David Lubin and
    Marilyn Langfeld: Community
    Type & Design, San Rafael,
    California
Printed and bound by Kingsport
    Press, Kingsport, Tennessee

3010-28.
22-32

9148